THE **PRICE**

THE
PRICE

MATTHEW BARROW

Troubador Publishing Ltd
Unit E2 Airfield Business Park,
Harrison Road, Market Harborough,
Leicestershire LE16 7UL
Tel: 0116 279 2299
Email: books@troubador.co.uk
Web: www.troubador.co.uk

ISBN 978-1-80514-296-6

British Library Cataloguing in Publication Data.
A catalogue record for this book is available from the British Library.

Printed and bound in Great Britain by 4edge Limited
Typeset in 11pt Minion Pro by Troubador Publishing Ltd, Leicester, UK

For Jatinder

CONTENTS

1. KRYSTAN

One week after his thirtieth birthday, Krystan Hoad had a call from his line manager. It was unusual for her to call him directly like that and, when her face appeared on the screen, she looked serious. It was only 9.30 in the morning and the day was just getting started.

'Krystan,' Una said simply. 'Can you come up to Fraser's office?'

'Now?'

'Yes please.' She smiled very briefly and uncomfortably. 'See you in a minute.'

She disappeared and Krystan stared at the blank screen. Fraser was Director of Data, the second highest of all of his bosses. Why would he want to see Krystan? Or did Una have something to tell him and was just borrowing Fraser's room? There was only one way to find out.

Krystan's desk was in a large open plan office with a hundred other desks and people coming and going all the time, so nobody particularly noticed or cared when he got up and walked away. He was based on the third floor and Fraser's office was on the eighth. The elevator was empty apart from a catering robot carrying a tray of defrosting vol-au-vents.

'You going up or down?' Krystan asked the robot.

'Up,' it said. 'Sixth floor.'

Krystan stepped inside and said, 'Sixth floor, eighth floor.'

As they moved, Krystan looked at his clean-shaven, slight-framed self in the reflection of the lift's mirrored back wall. The robot left with its vol-au-vents at the sixth, which had most of the conference rooms. On the eighth floor the elevator opened into a waiting area with corridors coming off it to the left and right. Krystan turned left and stopped at a door stencilled with Fraser's name. He knocked.

'Come in,' Una's voice said.

There was a round meeting table straight ahead as he walked in and that was where Krystan found Fraser, Una, a third man he didn't recognise, and an armed android with bulky shoulders and no face. A single blue screen sat in the centre of its head. The humans were sitting, but the android stood to attention beside the unknown man. The atmosphere was very serious. Krystan closed the door behind him.

'Krystan, come in,' Fraser said. He was older than Krystan, somewhere in his fifties, with a deep, warm voice that carried natural authority. 'Take a seat.' Krystan walked towards them, looking questioningly at Una, who was about his own age and who was looking nervous and upset. He sat down and noticed how much nicer the chair was than the chairs in normal meeting rooms.

'This is Mr. Beck,' Fraser said. 'From the Department of Citizenship.'

'Hello,' Krystan said. Mr. Beck nodded.

'Krystan,' Fraser said. 'I'm afraid I have some difficult news. This morning we are going to have to make some redundancies at the officer level, effective immediately. I'm sorry to say that your role is going to be closed.'

Krystan stared at him.

'Redundancies?'

'Yes.'

'How many?'

'Thirty.'

'Why?'

'Budget cuts, primarily,' Fraser said. 'Efficiency savings.'

Krystan looked at Una, then at Mr. Beck, then at the android.

'Why mine?'

'We've cut ten data officer positions. They were selected randomly.'

'Would you like some water?' Una said. She pushed a small plastic beaker towards him. Krystan picked it up and took small sips. His heart was racing and he didn't know what to think. He said,

'Effective immediately?'

'I'm afraid so. We need you to leave the building this morning.'

For a moment Krystan said nothing. Then he asked them:

'Who else is going?'

'There will be a meeting at eleven when everyone affected and their line managers will be told, and there will be an office-wide announcement immediately after that.'

Something wasn't adding up.

'So why are you telling me separately?' Krystan asked.

Fraser turned to Mr. Beck. The government official was a similar age to Fraser and had the look of someone who was used to delivering bad news – and who knew his authority was beyond question.

'Mr. Hoad,' Mr. Beck said. 'Coincidental to your redundancy, you have been assigned to pay the Price.'

Krystan's heart froze. A huge 'No!' rose up within him.

'No,' he said aloud.

'Yes, Mr. Hoad.'

'That's impossible.'

Mr. Beck had no need to argue.

'You have been assigned to pay the Price,' he repeated. 'It will take effect in seven days, on Sunday the sixteenth of February.' He pushed a small booklet across the table. 'This document explains how your new status will be processed, what will become of your assets, and so on. Most of it will be enacted by government, there is very little that you need to do.'

Krystan picked up the booklet and looked at its cover blankly. It was called *Paying the Price: A Guide*. He flicked through its pages but couldn't take in a word. He looked at Una pleadingly. 'There must be something,' he began, but then turned to Mr. Beck instead. Una was silent and tearful.

'Why does it have to be me?' Krystan said.

'Why does it have to be anyone?' Mr. Beck replied. 'You know how the Price works, Mr. Hoad.'

'I'm sorry, Krystan,' Fraser added.

*

Obediently, Krystan cleared his desk and left the building before 10.30. A security droid accompanied him, and because of that no one asked him any questions. Some watched as he filled his bag, and he could see that Clemmie was dying to ask him what was going on. When the other redundancies came later that morning, it wouldn't be like this – it would be a communal event, and amid all the shock there would be goodbyes and sympathy and 'keep in touch' and even 'I know a job you could apply for.' And there would be general anger at the company for making the cuts and channels for expressing and containing it. Krystan was leaving in the way he was, quietly and alone, because he was paying the Price. Later on, somehow or other, people would be told that he had joined the twenty per cent. And once they learned that, they would never call him.

He spent the rest of the day in a daze. He sat on a bench in a small park and read some of the booklet. He would have to leave the flat and move to a payer area – the booklet listed which areas he could live in. He would be allowed to keep a small portion of his savings, but the rest would be confiscated. The booklet gave a list of the jobs he could do, but he couldn't bring himself to look at that yet. He gazed around the green of the park. Was anyone here paying the Price? He doubted it, though there was one elderly woman whose clothes suggested she might be.

5

At midday he ate his sandwiches on the bench, then spent the afternoon wandering aimlessly around town. As the working day drew to a close, he gravitated towards Glynis's office. He had wanted to call her right away but didn't dare because he didn't know if he was being watched or what would happen to her if a payer called her at work. As 5.30 came close, he went into a café opposite her building and bought a cup of tea while he could still afford it. By now it was getting dark and the long evening had begun. He watched the warm lights of office windows and passing cars.

He texted to tell her where he was waiting, and at 5.40 she walked through the café doors to where he sat by the window. She was two years younger than Krystan and always looked as though she had got dressed in a hurry. 'This is a nice surprise!' she said, but he got to his feet and led her straight back outdoors. Her smile dropped. Outside, he took her hand and they started walking.

'What's wrong?' Glynis said.

Krystan was leading her to a park about ten minutes away. He didn't want to say too much while they could be overheard, so he just told her about the redundancy.

'Oh no!' she cried out. 'What happened?'

'Cuts,' he said. To kill time he told her about the thirty people, the group announcement, the clear-your-desk-today deadline – all as though he were one of the thirty. By the time he was finished they were in the park and sitting on a bench under a large cedar tree. He took a deep breath.

'But I was told before everyone else,' he added.

'Were you?'

'I was called up to Fraser Roberts's office to see him and Una, and they told me.'

6

Glynis was puzzled.

'There was another guy there,' he went on, 'and a security robot. They said I have to pay the Price.'

The colour drained from Glynis's face.

'What?' she said quietly.

'I'm paying the Price,' Krystan repeated.

Tearful, frightened, Glynis began to explain why that was completely impossible and must be some kind of mistake. Krystan showed her the booklet and told her what Mr. Beck had said. But still Glynis struggled to believe it. She asked him what Mr. Beck's exact words had been, and if there was any way he could have misunderstood them. But there was no doubt.

'I have to pay the Price,' Krystan told her again.

They wanted to walk. They left the park and, as they went, began thinking aloud – Glynis first, then Krystan – about what they could do, who they could turn to. They wondered if they could appeal, or somehow stop it from happening, and if they couldn't stop it, then what would happen to them? They talked about calling his parents, her parents, her uncle who was high up in Central Bank, his brother Sanford who was a communist (or something). But apart from Sanford, none of those people could help, and Sanford could only help in that he would tell them how to join a revolutionary commune and reject the system, which hardly seemed a help at all. They didn't want to contact their parents because they were scared of dragging them down with them, and in talking about that they realised that they didn't really understand how the Price worked, because it was something that happened to other people.

'What are we going to do?' Glynis said. Krystan held her tight in the middle of the street and said, 'It's just me, Glee, I won't let it affect you,' and she replied, 'Oh no, this is us.' They left it at that, but within himself Krystan was miserably resolved that he might lose Glynis too, if the alternative was taking her down with him.

Eventually, exhausted, they decided that they needed to be alone and they needed to understand what was happening better – so they headed back to their flat, walking all the way even though their feet were hurting, to get some food inside them and read the booklet properly. Krystan made some toast – it was all they could face – and they curled up side by side on the sofa. Glynis opened the booklet. She read silently for a few seconds.

'Have you seen the introduction?' she said.

'No.'

She held it up.

'This little paragraph on the first page.' She started to read. '"Equality is impossible. In order to neutralise the instability and insecurity caused by inequality and in order to ensure a high standard of living for the majority, the government seeks to contain inequality rather than eliminate it. The tool for containing inequality is the Price. In order for the majority to live well, a minority must live less well. Citizens who pay that Price are selected arbitrarily across all characteristics by government. Thanks to these selections, all citizens know where they stand and society remains stable. By this method, a majority are guaranteed a high standard of living and all of society is guaranteed order."'

It was a long time since they had heard the Price

summarised like that – not since they were at school, in fact. People just did not talk about the Price. That was the point of it, that was evidence, in a way, of its effectiveness: people knew it was there, knew that there were citizens and payers, knew that this was decided by automated arbitrary selection, and did not need to think about it further. Although Krystan understood that the Price was paid randomly, deep down he'd always felt that there was some reason to it, some fairness or rightness. Some people paid the Price, people he didn't know, and somehow that was their responsibility, or their fate, or in their nature. Paying the Price belonged to them, that was their place in the world. But now, now that it was happening to him, he suddenly saw the cold unfairness of it.

They read through the booklet. There were chapters on Employment and Earnings, Savings, Healthcare, Travel Restrictions, and The Police and Your Rights. Every chapter basically boiled down to a description of what you were no longer allowed to do or no longer allowed to have. The last chapter was on Price Avoidance. The penalties were severe.

Glynis held the booklet in her hands and Krystan read over her shoulder. It was her way of carrying the burden for him, of looking after him. But when they were through, Krystan lifted it from her fingers and held it in his lap, gazing at its cover.

'So we have seven days,' Glynis said. The flat was rented in both their names. According to the booklet, the contract would automatically move to Glynis alone and Krystan had to move out. The value of what possessions he could keep was capped, but there was nothing expensive he would have taken anyway. The main question was where he would go.

'I could stay with Sanford,' Krystan said.

'Sanford, really?'

'He'd take me in, and he lives in Turpin, which is allowed.'

'Are you allowed to live with him?' Glynis said hesitantly.

Krystan waved the booklet.

'It doesn't say who you can live with, only where. I suppose they don't think too much about ordinary people living in payer areas.'

He shifted in his seat, moving closer to Glynis.

'I could become a revolutionary like Sanford,' he said. 'I could join that group he's in.' Glynis couldn't tell if he was joking. She noticed that he was talking about himself, not them both, but she let it pass. He was thinking things through, looking for ways to survive. She said:

'What would that mean, though?'

He shrugged.

'I don't know. Live with Sanford… live in a commune. I don't know anything about them really.' He took her hands in his. 'What about you?' He cast his eyes around the room. 'I could live here in secret. Or you could come… no.' Things were starting to seem impractical, now that he had remembered her. 'How would we do it? I wonder what life is like in Turpin. What job could I do? Even if I became a revolutionary, I'd still need a job. What do you think? Maybe it wouldn't be so bad… maybe you can make an okay life for yourself if you live modestly. Payers have families, it can't be horrible all the time…'

'It's a very hard life,' Glynis said.

'You can make the most of it. Maybe it would be okay. Maybe I could slowly try to rebuild my life and find a way back. Maybe there's a way round it if you show you're hard working… maybe you can save in secret, maybe there's a black market in coming back… or maybe…'

He went quiet.

'What?'

'What if it's right, and it just happens to be me who pays? Maybe that's fair enough. I mean, why not me?'

'No…'

'You could see it as a good thing… one of the people who pays the Price for the good of society. You could take pride in it. People should respect payers because they make everything else possible.'

'Krystan.' Glynis didn't like the way this was going.

'There are more important things than money and status and material things,' Krystan said. 'Maybe it'll help me see what really matters in life, you know. The deeper values in life. I can live a good life and not set too much store on money and status and things like that.'

'You don't have to pay the Price to do that,' Glynis said. 'Anyway, Sanford lives like that and he fights the Price.' She was turning his mind back to Sanford not because she believed in his revolution but because she wanted Krystan in a defiant, self-respecting state of mind, not accepting being pushed to the bottom.

'That's true,' Krystan said slowly.

Glynis made a decision.

'I think we should go and see Sanford,' she said. 'Tomorrow.'

'Really?'

'He'll know what to do, he knows all about how the system works. He'll help us, like you said. We've got a week to sort it out. I'll call in sick.'

'Shall I call him now?'

'No,' Glynis said. 'They might be listening.'

*

The next morning they took the bus, which made the journey three times as long but meant they avoided the subway's surveillance cameras, which were more effective than those outdoors. There were a few spy drones in the streets, but unless one of them was following you specifically, they generally didn't take in anything. Krystan and Glynis had no idea whether paying the Price, or transferring into paying the Price, brought more surveillance, but it seemed like a natural consequence.

It took just over two hours to get to Turpin. Its edges, where Sanford lived, weren't too bad: ordinary citizens as well as payers lived there, and it wasn't until you reached the centre that you saw the real hardship. Sanford lived on the second floor of a scruffy ten storey block. It had been a while since Krystan and Glynis last came here. Outside the block the plain silver disc of a single drone hovered above the entrance with no obvious purpose.

Krystan pressed the buzzer. There was no answer. They waited.

'Maybe he's out,' Glynis said.

Krystan pressed the buzzer again. Finally a wary voice said:

'Who is it?'

'It's Krystan. And Glee.'

'Krystan?'

'Yeah!'

The door to the block abruptly opened with a primitive click. They walked up two flights of concrete steps to find a thin young man with shoulder length hair and wearing a scruffy t-shirt waiting for them in a doorway.

'What's wrong?' he asked them.

'Why does something have to be wrong?' Krystan said to his younger brother. But Sanford just looked suspicious. 'Can we come in?' Krystan added.

Sanford stepped aside so they could enter. He led them through a short, narrow hallway to a living room with a sofa and three wooden chairs. His flat was small and cluttered with books and pamphlets. A synthesizer keyboard leaned on its side against one wall, and there were stacks of books by revolutionary types they had suffered Sanford talking about for years. They stood uncertainly in the centre of the room.

'Are you okay?' Sanford said. 'Is it Mum and Dad?'

'Mum and Dad are fine,' Krystan told him.

'Can we sit down?' Glynis asked.

Sanford waved at the sofa but remained standing.

'Why didn't you call?' he said.

His visitors sat down. Krystan cut straight to it.

'I didn't want the government to trace it. I lost my job yesterday. They said I have to pay the Price.'

'What?'

'A guy was there from the Ministry of Citizenship. He said I've been assigned to pay the Price and it starts in seven days.'

13

Sanford turned to Glynis as though with a question, then back to his brother. 'Just you?'

'Yeah.'

'What did he say, exactly?'

Krystan gave him the full account: summoned to Fraser's office by Una; Mr. Beck and the armed android; the thirty redundancies; the booklet; clearing his desk. As Krystan spoke, Sanford sat on one of the wooden chairs, listening intently. His ears pricked up at the mention of the booklet. When the story was over, he was quiet for a while. They waited. He said:

'So you were the only payer out of the thirty.'

'I think so. I don't know what to do,' Krystan added abruptly. 'We didn't know… we thought you might know what we should do.'

'I can help you,' Sanford said quickly. He sounded upset, in a way they were not used to with him. 'I'm not… the River of Life can help you. I'll call someone.' He turned to the window. 'Did anyone follow you here?'

Krystan and Glynis exchanged glances, alarmed.

'I don't think so,' Krystan said.

'Any drones?'

'No…'

'There's a drone outside,' Glynis offered.

'That's always there', Sanford said. 'Actually that's a good point, what difference does it make? They know you've come to see me now.'

'You're under surveillance?'

'Everyone's under surveillance.'

'What's the River of Life?' asked Glynis.

'The River of Life is a network of payers who look out

for each other. They pool resources and club together. I can get you into it.'

Krystan looked at his brother.

'Is that what I have to do?'

'What?'

'Can't I get out of it?'

'What, the Price?'

'Yes!'

Sanford breathed heavily.

'Sorry, Krys… the Price shuts you out, that's what it is. You can't get round it.'

'What about a fake ID or something?'

Sanford shook his head.

'That never works.'

Glynis put her arm around Krystan's shoulders. Suddenly Sanford said, as though changing the subject:

'Have you got the booklet on you?'

Surprised, Krystan rifled through his small rucksack and handed over the *Guide*. Sanford flicked though its pages critically.

'Still the twenty-first edition,' he said. 'This is about a year old.'

'You know it?'

Sanford gestured towards the bottom of a short bookshelf beside the TV, to a row of tatty booklets of various sizes and colours.

'I've got every edition, going back fifty years.'

'But the Price is older than – ' Glynis began.

'They didn't do the guide at first,' Sanford interrupted her. 'They started it later, over a decade after the cull.'

Glynis winced at calling it 'the cull', though she knew

the term was common among those who thought as Sanford did. When they had learned about the Price at school, and on the rare occasions when any regular citizen referred to it, the beginning of the Price was called 'the Designation'.

Sanford watched his brother. 'Are you okay?'

Krystan didn't answer.

'We thought maybe Krystan could live with you,' Glynis said.

'Yes, you can, but... you can stay with me for a bit, but payers living with citizens is risky. You'll need your own place.'

'What about Glee?' Krystan asked.

'That's...' He faltered.

Krystan looked in agony at his brother. 'They're taking everything!'

Glynis leaned into him and held his arms.

'They're not taking me.'

'They can't take everything,' said Sanford. 'They can't do that. You've got me, you've got Glynis, and there are others. Trust me, Krys,' he said. 'It's not over.'

2. GLYNIS

Two weeks after Krystan was assigned to pay the Price, Glynis Thorley had a call from her line manager. Glynis shared a small office with four other people, but Betsy had a separate room down the corridor. A message popped up on Glynis's screen: *Hi Glynis, are you free to pop over to my office for a quick chat?*

It was unusual because normally when Betsy wanted a quick chat, she would just wander down to the office. If it happened the other way round, with Betsy calling you to her, it meant it was something either personal or serious. The moment Glynis saw the message she felt a stab of cold. There was only one serious thing on her mind these days, and she knew that sooner or later the news was going to reach work. Was this it?

There was only one way to find out. Glynis put down her coffee and got up from her chair. No one asked her where she was going. She walked out of the office and turned left down the narrow, blue carpeted corridor to the office that Betsy shared with Skylar. The door was ajar and Glynis could see that Skylar wasn't there – instead, a round-faced man who was difficult to age sat opposite Betsy's desk, talking quietly. Glynis tapped on the door.

'Hi, Glynis – come in,' Betsy said. 'Could you close the door behind you?'

Betsy was only a year older than Glynis and spoke as though she was not senior, but had a quality to her manner that made it clear she very definitely was senior. Glynis walked hesitantly into the room. The man smiled.

'This is Bob,' said Betsy. 'From HR.'

'How do you do,' said Bob.

'Hello,' Glynis said warily.

'Sit down,' Betsy invited her.

She sat next to Bob. Betsy leaned her elbows on the desk and looked at Glynis with concern.

'How are things?' she said. 'Is everything alright?'

'Fine,' Glynis said. 'I'm fine, thanks.'

Betsy looked at Bob.

'You've moved house,' she said.

This was it. Glynis shifted in her chair.

'Yes,' she said. 'A couple of days ago.'

'To Turpin, is that right?' Betsy asked innocently.

'That's right.'

Bob coughed slightly.

'That's an interesting choice,' he said. 'Isn't Turpin a payer area?'

'Not exclusively,' Glynis told him.

'No, not exclusively. But largely.'

'Yes.'

'Is there any particular reason you chose to move to a payer area?' he asked her.

Glynis didn't answer right away.

'Personal reasons,' she said.

'Personal reasons,' he repeated.

'Yes.' She locked eyes with him for a second with a little dose of defiance. She had a right to privacy, legally speaking, even if in practice there was little actual privacy. They could spy on her, but they couldn't make her tell them anything.

'Your partner,' Betsy said quietly. 'Krystan. Isn't he – wasn't he recently assigned to pay the Price?'

Glynis blushed a little, annoyed that it embarrassed her.

'Yes – he was told two weeks ago.'

'He lives in Turpin too,' Bob said.

'Not with me.'

Bob smiled.

'No, of course.'

'We're a little concerned, Glynis,' Betsy said. 'I'm sure you can understand that the Department would be concerned that a government employee moves to a payer area two weeks after her partner becomes... pays the Price.'

'It's not against the law,' Glynis said.

Betsy looked taken aback.

'No, no – of course not. But blurring the line between payers and citizens... it's a bit of a tightrope, isn't it. And there are, um, seditious groups that live along the, um, those blurred edges. I'm sure you can understand that the Department would be concerned that a government employee is moving closer to those... margins.'

'Do you think I should leave him?' Glynis snapped.

Now Betsy blushed. She sat back in her chair.

'That's not for me to – '

'We just want to check in with you, Glynis,' Bob said. 'To let you know that the Department has concerns and that if at any time you need any advice or support, we're here. You can talk to Betsy at any time, or you can approach HR directly if you prefer.'

'Okay,' Glynis said.

'But it's only fair to make you aware that the Department is monitoring the situation,' Bob added.

'Okay,' Glynis said again.

'How is Krystan?' Bob asked her.

She didn't answer. Bob and Betsy exchanged a glance. Bob said, 'Thank you, Glynis. That was all we wanted to say.'

Glynis left the room without another word. Back at her desk, she wanted to talk to Krystan, or Sanford, but didn't dare. It would have to wait.

*

The rest of the day passed like any other. At 6.00 Glynis gathered her coat and bag and popped her head round Betsy's door to say goodnight just as she always did, and Betsy smiled goodnight in return as though nothing was up, and Glynis headed home. It was already dark outside. She walked the ten minutes to Westminster station and caught the Jubilee Line and then the Southern Line all the way to Turpin. After a short while the train all but emptied and Glynis could settle into a seat and into her book, an old tract called *Frames* that Sanford had given her. A lot of it was history, but history she had never heard before. She wasn't sure how much to believe.

Her phone buzzed. It was a message from Krystan telling her that he was not at the Y. Krystan not being at the Y was code for him being at Rawlins Books. Glynis replied with a simple *okay* and as she put her phone back in her bag, she noticed an android standing at the far end of the carriage. It was tall and heavy, a dull matt grey and very functional-looking, the kind of android that worked in warehouses or construction sites. There was nothing particularly unusual about it, but after this morning Glynis felt… wary. It was facing away from her but that meant nothing. The eyes in an android's face were not its only way of looking.

When she stepped off the train at Turpin Station, the android left with her. Glynis hesitated before walking her usual route along the tiled corridor to the escalator and then taking a second escalator to ground level. The android was right behind her, never close but never out of sight. There were only two routes out of Turpin Station so this still wasn't unusual. The exit was staffed by a bored woman standing sentry by the ticket machine and one of the squat, rust-coloured 'grumpy' robots that you got at every tube station, with a cube for a head, a larger cube for a body and a grill for a face. Glynis passed through the gate and out into the dark, cold streets of Turpin, busy with people, bars, and a corner shop and bakery that were still open. Drones passed overhead, doing who knew what, belonging to who knew who. Drones had been a minor presence in Glynis's life until now – in Turpin they were everywhere. She paused outside the station for a minute and the warehouse android didn't overtake her. Then she turned left and walked quickly.

Rawlins Books was twenty minutes away. Halfway, Glynis paused at a C&A to look in the window and briefly glanced back. The android was behind her, quite a way behind, and had stopped dead in the middle of the pavement. It wasn't doing anything and nobody was paying it any attention. She went on her way.

The bookstore was open late every weekday, and Krystan and Sanford had begun hanging out in the Movies section at the back. It was a large store, warm and quiet with tall shelves and a little café off to the side. Glynis walked straight to the back without talking to or acknowledging anyone. She found Krystan and Sanford exactly where she expected to find them and with them was Ottoline, a young member of Sanford's group who worked at the shop. She was tidying the shelves and chatting to the other two as they flicked through a photobook about the making of *Logan's Run*. It was Ottoline who noticed Glynis first.

'Is there an android behind me?' Glynis asked abruptly.

All three looked over her shoulder.

'No,' Krystan told her.

But they saw the worry in Glynis's face.

'I'll take a look outside,' said Ottoline and headed quickly for the front.

'Were you being followed?' Krystan asked her.

'I don't know. It was on the tube and then it was behind me all the way here. It was just a manual but – '

'It doesn't matter what it looked like,' Sanford said.

Ottoline was already coming back. She was short, not much over five feet, and wore a faux-leather motorbike jacket everywhere she went, though she didn't ride a motorbike.

'There's a grey manual outside, looking at the traffic,' she said.

Now Glynis looked scared. She turned to Krystan.

'It followed me from work. I had a meeting today,' she said, and told them about her chat with Betsy and Bob.

'Let's go and talk to it,' said Sanford.

'What?'

'They don't like being brought into the open,' he said. 'In spite of everything, they're more scared of the people than you think.'

'No, Sanford,' Krystan told him.

'You don't have to come,' Sanford said. 'I'll just ask it what it's doing.'

He headed for the front of the store. Ottoline followed him. Krystan and Glynis looked at each other.

'We might as well,' Glynis said.

They followed Sanford and Ottoline outside. Sanford was standing beside the android, looking up at it as it stared blankly into the road.

'Hello,' Sanford said.

Androids – all androids – were obliged by programming to acknowledge human beings. It turned its head.

'How can I help you?' it said. Its voice was smooth and male.

'What are you doing?' Sanford asked it.

'I am waiting for instructions.'

'What are you doing *here*?'

The android did not hesitate. It was perfectly capable of lying.

'I have made a delivery,' it said.

'Where to?'

Now there was a pause as the robot searched its database for a plausible location.

'The Grove Public House,' it said. 'I delivered a crate of beers that was omitted from a previous delivery.'

The Grove was two minutes away. There was no point in going there to get the story verified because if an android walked into a pub in Turpin and lied in front of the staff about having just made a delivery, the staff would only confirm the lie.

'Why don't you know what to do next?' Sanford asked it. 'Why are you still waiting for instructions?'

That was a very good question. The android took a moment to find a reply.

'Other units are making similar supplementary deliveries in this area. There is a delay in co-ordination, and I am waiting for instructions to either return to base or perform another task.'

'How long will that take?'

Instantly the robot said:

'I have received instructions. Excuse me.'

It turned and walked away, back the way it had come.

Sanford turned to the others.

'See? It lied. If they weren't afraid, it wouldn't lie. It would tell me to mind my own business.'

'Are you sure about that?' Glynis asked him.

'They basically told you this morning they're watching you, but they half-pretend they're not. They want you to know, but they don't want to admit it. They want to scare you, but you're still a citizen and citizens still have rights, more or less.'

Glynis was doubtful. Sanford was very sure about a lot of things, but she and Krystan were not sure of anything.

'If you say so,' she said.

'I'm cold,' said Ottoline. 'Come inside, I'll make some hot chocolate.'

*

The River of Life's solution to the poverty of paying the Price was communal living. Sanford had found Krystan a place in a small house with three other people: Audrey, roughly his own age; Darcy, a woman in her mid-forties; and Harry, in his late fifties. All of Krystan's new housemates were born payers, and Harry in particular had suffered a rough time, homeless for a while and spending time in jail before finding the River of Life. Audrey was a bag of nerves who looked as though she wanted to flee every conversation, but Darcy was lively and full of certainty, unshakeable in her opposition to the Party of Order and Nation and its government. Like Sanford and Ottoline, she was a member of the Dream League, a resistance group connected to the River of Life.

After the altercation with the android, Glynis, Krystan, Sanford and Ottoline walked the half hour to Krystan's house and settled in the kitchen with Harry and Darcy. They stood in the thin galley, leaning against the worktop, sink, stove and windowsill, sipping tea and talking over what had happened. Darcy was sure that Glynis was about to lose her job.

'You're a proper lender now,' she said. It was a congratulation, not a regret. A lender was a term some used for those who had voluntarily joined the payer world to some degree and ended up half-paying alongside them, the only difference being that they had a way back to citizenship if they wanted it. Glynis had heard the term a lot in the past two weeks. Sanford and Ottoline were both lenders.

'I guess I'll see on Monday,' Glynis said.

'It's intimidation,' said Harry. He looked at Sanford. 'Sending a big robot like that. Why do you think they did that?'

Sanford shrugged.

'They want to scare Glee into turning back,' he said. 'They're hoping a demonstration like that will keep her at home.'

'Huh.'

'I think so too,' Darcy said. 'It was their last warning. A little taste of life on the outside.'

'So do you think they'll do it again?' Glynis asked them.

'I doubt it,' Ottoline said. 'Not after we talked to the android. But they'll keep watching you, like they watch all of us.' She turned to the ceiling as though there was something there. 'Maybe not a drone yet, but bugs.'

'This house isn't bugged,' Harry said. 'I sweep it every week.'

'Drones, yes,' Darcy said thoughtfully. 'There's always drones.'

'It's nothing to worry about,' Sanford told Glynis. 'They'll watch but they won't do anything.'

'But no more androids,' Glynis concluded hopefully.

'No more androids,' Sanford confirmed. 'I mean I doubt it.'

'They might send police,' Darcy said. 'Would police bother you?'

'I haven't done anything illegal,' Glynis said, something she reminded herself of a lot lately.

'Not yet,' Darcy added.

'The police aren't going to change my mind.' She moved closer to Krystan.

'Well then the police are unlikely to bother you,' Darcy said. 'With you having a government job, I think the state profilers will know you pretty well.'

*

They ended up staying late at Krystan's, so that in the end Ottoline and Sanford crashed on the floor of Krystan's small room. The next morning they rose early because Krystan had to go to work. The River of Life had quickly helped him get a job at a Berets warehouse. The pay wasn't as low as some and the hours weren't too bad, and some of the local managers were sympathetic to the (illegal) unions. Krystan was lucky. Because of Sanford he had gone from paying the Price straight into the arms of the River and the League, bypassing the worst of payer life and held up by the resistance. He knew how fortunate he was; Sanford made it clear, and the more Krystan and Glynis learned, the more they could see it for themselves. He had had a soft landing.

But this weekend, that soft landing included a Saturday shift and he had to get going, so he kissed Glynis goodbye and left the three of them standing outside the house. Sanford took Glynis and Ottoline to a café and treated them to breakfast. Glynis found it hard to keep from looking at the drones that hung overhead, trying to work out if any were watching her in particular. But it was impossible to tell.

Krystan's shift was all day and Glynis wouldn't see him until the evening, so after breakfast she went with the other two to a Dream League meeting held at a flat belonging to someone called Ravi Babbington, a leading light in the League's organisation. The flat was in Lethbridge, a relatively affluent citizen area that sat right alongside Turpin. Ravi Babbington was neither a payer nor a lender. Sanford and Ottoline didn't know much about her – she was a wealthy benefactor who opposed the Price, and she assisted the League by letting them use her flat and by helping them organise – but she never, in any way that could be recorded, gave them money. That was the loophole that kept her on the right side of the law – that, and the fact that she was connected enough for the authorities to be reluctant to interfere with her.

On the way to Ravi's flat they were very definitely targeted by two drones that floated two metres above and three metres behind them for the entire walk. Whether they were there for Glynis or because the three of them were headed for a League meeting, they would never know. Perhaps it was both. The drones made no attempt to be discreet, and when they reached Ravi's building, they found eight more drones hovering outside. This was clearly a meeting to watch.

They entered a simple but elegant lobby after Sanford

tapped in a code at the building's entrance, and took a spacious elevator to the second floor. Ravi lived in Flat B4, down a short corridor with lavender walls. Ottoline knocked and a slight young woman in a baseball cap let them in. The flat was large, with a long, curved hallway that led them to a wide room where they found five League members and Ravi drinking tea and munching biscuits. Sanford and Ottoline introduced Glynis, who had only met one of them before, a fellow young lender called Fionnuala. Ravi herself was serious looking: somewhere around fifty, her hair was in a crew cut and she wore a dark blue shirt and black jeans. Glynis thought she would be intimidating, but once things got started, she turned out to be warm and self-effacing and spent most of the morning acting as administrator – although the meeting itself, when it eventually started, was a fairly unplanned affair.

The group spent a long time analysing Glynis's encounter with the android and her conversation with Betsy and Bob. When official business began, it was mostly about housekeeping, pamphlet printing (the League's core activity was the illegal distribution of pamphlets), and a demonstration in Parliament Square planned by Justice, a rival anti-Price movement. The demonstration had been legally permitted by the government, which made the League suspicious, but that wasn't their main problem with it – the real problem was an ideological difference with Justice that made some League members reluctant to join them. This difference, Glynis gathered, was that Justice opposed the Price but believed that where there was inequality, or even poverty, it should be based on

29

'real' or 'just' causes. The Dream League, on the other hand, did not believe that inequality needed to exist at all. As Sanford put it, Justice wanted to return to 'the old pre-Price illusions,' or 'the old world,' whereas the League wanted something new. But Justice was a larger and better resourced outfit – perhaps because their ideas had wider appeal, perhaps because their acceptance of rich and poor made them more palatable to the government. If the Price were ever overthrown, Sanford said, those at the top would find the Justice model one they could live with.

The meeting ended with Ravi suddenly holding forth about psychology. Whether this talk was a regular feature or a spontaneous musing, Glynis couldn't tell, but the group listened respectfully and only a couple intervened with their own observations. Ravi began with a potted history lesson: she talked about the Party of Order and Nation (the PON) coming to power almost eighty years ago after the chaos of the climate wars, elected by a people craving stability and security – 'order.' Right away the PON was authoritarian, but it didn't introduce the Price until a decade later, after successfully stamping its presence on the country and effectively neutering democracy. When the Price came – in the form of the cull, or 'the Designation' – it was quick and brutal: millions in an already economically battered country having most of what little they had stripped away, millions more being told the future was theirs. After that, the class of payers had been fairly static, in line with the promised order, though it did need occasional adjustments – to maintain the optimal number needed in that lower order (which fluctuated with general population changes and the economy) and to maintain the appearance of 'arbitrariness' (so that paying never became solely a consequence of birth).

That arbitrariness and the system of 'designation' or 'assignment' – individuals randomly targeted to pay – was what interested Ravi today, because of its effect on how people thought. We need to feel in control of our lives, she said, we need things to have a reason. If you think you can suddenly be sent to the bottom of society for no reason whatsoever, how do you cope with that, that nagging insecurity? Well, you persuade yourself that there is some meaning to it, somehow, and that it won't happen to you. You can't help but feel that paying the Price is deserved in some way, that it has something to do with payers' natures or behaviour. You think that if you work hard, if you make yourself indispensable, if you embed yourself in the security of a good job, and if you behave yourself, then the Price won't be asked of you. So you make sure your company needs you, you may even try to climb the ranks, and you think about the Price and those who pay it as little as possible. You trust that things are as they should be, that the government is taking care of everything, that all is… in order. Which was why, Ravi said, it was so hard to persuade people to think about the Price, let alone question it, let alone challenge it.

Glynis wasn't sure how convinced she was by this, but she saw something in it. She knew that she and Krystan had never given the Price much thought until now, and that they had even kept Sanford at arms length precisely because he kept talking about it – until Krystan had been told to pay and the bottom fell out of their world. Now they were questioning everything.

When she was finished, their host ended with a self-deprecating chuckle and announced it was time for lunch. Some of those gathered were payers – was it legal to invite payers into your home and feed them, Glynis wondered? Ravi, with ten surveillance drones hovering outside her window, either knew that it was or didn't care that it wasn't.

In any case, Glynis and her friends weren't staying – they had a chore to do. They said their goodbyes and walked back to Turpin, their two drones in tow (which kept them from talking about what they had just heard). They walked to Glynis's new flat on Turpin's edge, five minutes from the station. It was still full of boxes and they made a half-hearted attempt at unpacking. She had only slept here a couple of nights so far, but the plan was that she would live here in the week and stay with Krystan at the weekend – an arrangement that would just about keep her on the right side of the law. They put away some clothes, hooked up the TV and a stereo and sorted out the pots and pans. By then they'd had enough, so they headed instead to Sanford's, where they flicked through his mountain of political tracts and he held forth about his favourite philosophers until Ottoline got bored and told him to put some music on. They talked about what Glynis should do at work on Monday: what she should say if they questioned her, how to respond if they fired her. At 7.00, Krystan got back from work. The four of them had pizza and crashed in front of the TV, and at the end of the night they went their separate ways. Ottoline had church the next day and Sanford had rehearsals with a band he played keyboards for. A single drone followed Ottoline home and a single drone trailed Krystan and Glynis to Krystan's house; two drones spent the night outside Sanford's place.

On Sunday Glynis and Krystan spent the day walking along the Thames, a single drone playing gooseberry. They walked and talked together for the whole day, speaking in low tones and euphemisms, about the Price, about Sanford, about the Dream League and the people they had met, about life in the River of Life, about what they would do when Glynis lost her job – and about other, better things, like how and when they could move back in together, about the music Sanford liked that they had never heard of, about the new season of *Plant Life* and whether Jazz would end up with Sarita. As they came back into town, they even went window shopping, and Krystan bought Glynis a little fabric bracelet from a hippy shop. Then they went home, tired, ate some curry that Darcy had made and went to sleep early. And all day long a drone followed them, two metres above and three metres behind. And all night, that drone hovered outside Krystan's window and monitored.

*

On Monday morning Glynis went to work early, at the same time as Krystan, and caught a quiet, pre-commuter tube into the city. She bought a coffee and sat in the park for a while, watching the squirrels and trying not to think. When she walked to the office, she found it empty apart from Ian, already absorbed in his screen. Glynis logged on, checked her messages and gazed idly at her To Do list. Betsy arrived at 8.50, popped her head round the door, clocked Glynis, looked surprised, and disappeared. The sacking came twenty minutes later. It began exactly like

Friday. A message popped up on Glynis's monitor: *Hi Glynis, are you free to pop over to my office?*

Missing this time was *for a quick chat.* There was not going to be a chat. Glynis packed her bag and even switched off her computer. She walked into Betsy's office carrying her jacket over her arm. Bob was there, in the same chair as last time, and next to him stood a blue-faced android with DC13A2 written on a small, square plate on its chest.

Bob looked serious.

'Hi Glynis. Close the door,' Betsy said. Her voice was warm but she was unsmiling. Glynis did as she was told and hesitated by the chair until Betsy indicated that she should sit. It wasn't until then that Glynis noticed how shaken Betsy was. How hard did she find this?

Bob did the talking.

'Glynis, some information has come to our attention.'

Glynis waited.

'You are involved with an organisation called the Dream League,' Bob continued.

'I went to a meeting on Saturday,' Glynis confirmed. She had discussed this with Sanford and Ottoline. Deny nothing that you know they know.

'The Dream League is an anti-government organisation,' Bob told her.

'It's anti-Price,' Glynis corrected him. But they both knew that anti-Price meant anti-government. She added, 'It's not proscribed.'

'It has not been outlawed – yet,' Bob conceded. 'But it's under surveillance and it's a Category Three organisation,' he said, as though she might not have realised that and might reconsider her actions now that she did. 'It's against the Civil Service code for employees to associate with Category Three organisations,' he added. 'It's a dismissible offence.'

Glynis's heart was racing. She looked at Betsy, but Betsy was avoiding her gaze and fixing her eyes squarely on Bob.

'Okay,' Glynis said quietly.

'We're going to have to let you go,' Bob told her. 'I'm sorry, Glynis.'

'That's okay,' Glynis told him.

*

She went back to the park with a few trinkets she'd retrieved from her desk (she'd been removing her things for a week, in preparation, and only had a few of the most conspicuous objects left). As soon as she sat on the bench she burst into tears. She called Krystan. It was safe enough because making the call told them nothing, confirmed nothing that they didn't already know. She talked for as long as it took to calm herself down, walking out of the park and hanging up when she reached the tube station. A single drone followed and abandoned her as she went inside. She took the tube straight to Turpin, and as soon as she left Turpin Station, a new drone made a beeline for her. Glynis stared straight at it for a long moment before going on her way, the drone trailing her like an obedient puppy. She walked straight to Rawlins Books. At the front desk she found Mr. Rawlins himself – a tall, older man who wore felt-like shirts and had short, pure grey hair. He smiled as she entered the shop.

'Hello, Glynis,' he said. 'Everything okay?'

'Hi, Mr. Rawlins,' she said as casually as she could manage. 'I'm looking for Ottoline.'

Mr. Rawlins pointed across the store. 'She's on café duty,' he said.

She found Ottoline clearing mugs from a table. The café was pretty quiet and there was just one other woman working there, in the little open kitchen. Ottoline hadn't seen Glynis coming and jumped a little when she heard her name.

'Hey,' she said when she recovered. Then she looked serious. 'You're not at work.'

'I got fired.'

Ottoline glanced across at Mr. Rawlins and sat at the table. Glynis joined her.

'How did they do it?' Ottoline said.

'I got called into Betsy's office. Bob from HR was there again with a security robot this time, he did all the talking. He said the League were a Category Three and it was a dismissible offence to mix with them.'

Ottoline had no experience of office life.

'And that was it?'

'That was it. I cleared my desk and came home.'

'Are you alright? Have you told Krystan?'

'I talked to him on the phone before I came home. I'm okay. Bit shaky.'

'Have a cup of tea,' Ottoline said and headed for the kitchen. Glynis followed her. The woman working there, Dana, could see they were having a private moment and vacated the spot without a word, moving seamlessly to replace Ottoline at the tables. Ottoline started making camomile tea. Glynis sat on a tall stool next to the sink.

'This is it,' Glynis said.

Ottoline nodded.

'This is it,' she agreed. 'You're out now. You're a revolutionary.'

Glynis laughed. She looked around at people quietly browsing books.

'I'm a revolutionary,' she repeated.

3. SANFORD

Three weeks after Glynis got fired, Sanford Hoad called on Ottoline at the bookstore. She wasn't working that day but it was their standard rendezvous. He found her in the café having toast for breakfast. Sanford sat opposite her at the little table and put his small rucksack on the floor between his feet. Ottoline was chatting to Dana. Sanford sat quietly until they had finished and Dana drifted back to work.

When Ottoline turned her attention to Sanford, the first thing she did was tap the little teapot in front of her and say, 'There's more in there if you want.'

'Go on then.' Sanford got up briefly to help himself to a mug behind the counter and poured himself some black tea. 'How long have you been here?'

'Twenty minutes.'

Sanford sipped his tea, but it was too hot. Ottoline pointed at the milk. He shook his head.

'What time is it now?' he asked.

Ottoline glanced at her phone.

'Ten exactly.'

'They'll be here in a minute.'

'Both of them? Is Krystan coming too?'

Sanford nodded.

'He's on nights this week.'

'Can I see a pamphlet?'

'Haven't you seen it yet?'

'Nope.'

Sanford reached into his rucksack and pulled out a thin, grey pamphlet. The cover was blank apart from the title: *The Truth About The Price*. Ottoline took it from him and thumbed through it.

'They were printed last week,' Sanford told her.

'I missed the meeting,' she reminded him. 'Did you write it?'

'Me and Brigitte.'

Ottoline read a few lines. Then she handed it back.

'Looks good,' she said, smiling.

Sanford laughed.

'Thanks.'

As he slotted the pamphlet back among the others, Krystan and Glynis appeared. Ottoline shuffled her chair so Glynis could sit beside her and Krystan sat next to his brother.

Glynis looked at Sanford. 'Is anyone else coming?'

'No, just us.'

'Your first pamphleteering,' Ottoline said.

'Exciting!' said Glynis.

'Have you got your masks?' Sanford asked her.

She reached into her jacket and dangled a standard nose-and-mouth health mask in the air.

'Yep!'

'And hats?'

'We have identical blue woollen hats,' she told him. 'His and hers!'

'That's a bit distinctive…' Sanford worried.

'It'll be fine,' Ottoline told him.

Sanford turned to his brother.

'You alright?'

'Not too bad,' Krystan said. He looked a little tired.

'What time's your shift tonight?' Sanford asked.

'Eight till eight.' Krystan said. He leaned forward, suddenly interested. 'We had an android malfunction yesterday. It dropped a crate and tried to pick up another robot. They stood there for ages stuck like sumo wrestlers. We called the engineers and they had to deactivate them. Apparently it happens every now and then, their object recognition goes off and needs resetting. But when they're deactivated, did you know they can still walk?'

'I've heard that,' Ottoline said.

'It's a factory setting. They follow a signal the engineers have and just walk back to the workshop. It's creepy.' He paused. 'It was sad to see really. I never paid much attention to androids before, but when you see them around a lot… you start to feel for them.'

'Do they have names?' Ottoline asked him.

'No.' Krystan shook his head. 'It's against the rules. But you can only tell them apart from little scratches and marks anyway, and Ghayth told me that every now and then they get buffed up and you can't tell them apart anymore.'

Glynis sighed.

'It seems sad,' she said.

'I'd never thought about it before,' Krystan told them. 'I mean everyone humanises robots a bit, but actually working with them, alongside them, it's different.'

'Only payers work alongside robots,' Sanford said, a little more bluntly than he meant to. 'I mean mostly.'

Krystan nodded thoughtfully.

'That's what it is,' he said.

They were quiet for a moment. Sanford finished his tea.

'Okay,' he said. 'Shall we go?'

*

They left the bookstore and turned off into Ransom Street. Five drones followed them. They avoided Turpin Station and walked instead to Gate Station just to throw the drones off a little. The walk took them through the outskirts of Gate district. It was a sunny March morning and people were strolling or hanging out in small, bored groups. Even though it was only the next area along, Gate was a place where movements like the River of Life were yet to gain a stronghold, and the impact of paying was not as softened as it was for many in Turpin. Launching into a history lesson, Sanford explained to Krystan and Glynis that Gate was taking longer to recover from the Brutalisation – the long period when the government actively suppressed communities for fear of those communities harbouring resistance. When the destruction of the Brutalisation became so visible that even the legal media began to talk about it, the government relaxed its grip and allowed selected charities to set up foodbanks and other forms of aid. What those charities discovered was already-existing, weak but determined secret movements holding things together, without whom the lives of those stuck in payer zones would have been crushed. As the government's grip loosened, those groups grew into 'the villages', as people called the River of Life and others: self-sufficient support networks that lightened the weight of paying. The past few years had seen a leap in the size of the villages, but still, progress was stifled by local corruption, organised crime and government interference.

Turpin, being a commercial area and close to non-paying boroughs with wealthy well-wishers, had been the quickest to build villages and was way ahead of its neighbours. Hence the ridiculous levels of surveillance there, the government's alternative to outright suppression. Gate, less accessible to citizen benefactors, more hampered by corruption, was slower. But it was making progress, one step at a time – and one sign of that was its own growth in surveillance. The five drones following Sanford and the others had plenty of company, including red drones, painted with red rectangles on their sides to signify that they were armed.

As they walked, Sanford and the gang acted out their alibi: flyposting. On Alton Road, Sanford reached into his rucksack and pulled out a handful of posters for his band The Thin Wall and gigs coming to the Suburbia club in May. Flyposting was illegal but nobody cared, least of all the drones. They stuck a couple of posters onto a bus stop and went on their way.

They kept this up for the whole walk, stopping every so often to slap a poster on a wall: partly ruse to throw the drones off the scent a little, partly genuine band promotion. At Gate Station Sanford shoved the remaining posters back into his bag and off they went, down the escalators and onto the Southern Line. They stood together at the far end of the platform. Their drones didn't follow because drones rarely entered buildings, even train stations. Inside, there were other ways of seeing.

They waited quietly on the dark platform, warily glancing at the few other passengers. The Southern Line mostly covered the less well off citizen parts of south London and skirted the payer boroughs, so once the commuting was done there was little reason to come here. While they waited, they put on their health masks. Health masks were less common at this time of year, but still used enough that they were not a suspicious thing to be wearing, and they made a handy disguise when you were doing something bordering on the illegal, like disseminating seditious material. Government controls were calibrated to not quite amount to a ban on free speech: criticism of the PON was permitted, questioning of the Price was permitted, and there was a fair amount of the former and occasionally, weakly, a little of the latter. It was all submerged by the sheer quantity of pro-government media, but it did happen. Subverting the social order and undermining the nation, however – that was illegal. What exactly crossed the line was ambiguous, and Sanford's pamphlet tried to be clever and keep on the right side of the law, but it was hard to be subtle when the entire order was what you were against. Sanford's calculation – the Dream League's calculation – was that arresting and punishing people for handing out a few pamphlets on a Monday morning when they could simply dismiss them as crackpots and extremists was just not worth the trouble. But it was worth it for the League. You had to start somewhere, and channels were limited. Some of Sanford's pamphlets would be picked up, and some of them would be read, and slowly and surely the League's message would spread.

A train pulled up, noisily, and the four revolutionaries stepped on board. The carriage was long and thin, with dark metal walls and dark blue seats facing each other across the aisle. Southern Line trains were always gloomy. There was only one other person in this carriage, a woman sat reading a tablet, a walking stick leaning low against her knees and stretching out to the seat opposite. As the train pulled away, they sat near the door, Krystan and Glynis on one side of the aisle, Sanford and Ottoline on the other.

Sanford pulled a pamphlet out of his bag and handed it to Ottoline, who pretended to read it. Sanford had a system, or ritual – in each train, he handed a single pamphlet to someone, they read it and then left it behind when they left. He had a notion that this threw the cameras off the scent, that it was more discrete than everyone carrying their own batch. People in the League even called it the 'Sanford system,' and the jury was out over how effective or necessary it was – mostly he got teased about it. But this was how Sanford liked to do it.

The four of them sat and chit-chatted as they would on any other trip into town. The train grated to a halt at the next stop, let two people in, and moved on. At the following stop the gang got up and left, Ottoline absently leaving her pamphlet on her seat. They walked along a short corridor to a new platform: Southern Line, southbound. This next train had more passengers scattered across the carriage and they could not all sit together, so Sanford sat with Glynis and handed her a pamphlet. They remained only until the next stop and as they left, Glynis dropped her pamphlet on her seat.

Back to the northbound line they went, this time staying put for seven stops, heading right into town, before it was Krystan's turn to leave his pamphlet behind. This was the day they had planned for themselves, back and forth on the Southern Line, dropping pamphlets. You wouldn't normally do this in groups of four, but this was a training day for Krystan and Glynis. It might look weird to anyone paying attention behind the surveillance cameras, this group moving erratically up and down the same line, but those spies were looking for crimes, public disturbances and named individuals rather than mere oddness: terrorism was not a significant problem in post-war, PON England. The bigger risk was the police spotting them with the pamphlets in person. But they had not seen any police that morning.

That wasn't to last. About an hour into their wearying routine (Sanford had committed them to two hours) a security android boarded their train one stop after they did. It stayed at the carriage's end, by the door – androids very rarely sat – and surveyed the passengers mechanically. It was pale blue, which meant it was police-endorsed – it held police authority and fed into the police database – but was not actually police: the kind of droid that businesses used internally. The tube used this kind of private security and actual police interchangeably; it was an opaque system. The gang kept their heads down. Sanford was already reading a pamphlet when the android boarded and he stayed in position, not wanting to look as though he was hiding something. They had planned to stay on this train for four stops. When Krystan glanced up, he was pretty sure the android was looking at his brother. It could see the pamphlet he held as plain as day.

At the next stop Krystan nudged Sanford's foot and said lightly, 'Off here?'

'Next one,' Sanford said and lowered the pamphlet, face down, as though he was tiring of reading. He looked along the carriage. If they didn't want to walk past the droid, the exit was a long stroll to the other end. As the train started moving again, Sanford waited for a minute and then said to the others, 'Next stop.'

He stood and made his way down the carriage. There were twenty-plus other people in this one, the busiest yet. The others followed him, stepping over people's feet and moving as though leisurely preparing to hop off at the next station. At one point, in spite of himself, Sanford looked back.

The android was following them.

Now his heart was suddenly racing. With an effort he kept to walking at the same pace, his eyes on the door ahead of him, his hand on the rail above to keep him upright as the train rocked mildly from side to side – his other hand holding his incriminating pamphlet.

Nearing the door, he stopped beside a man sitting on the end seat, in his fifties or sixties, with a brown briefcase lodged on the ground beneath his feet. As Sanford waited, the man caught his eye and smiled. The others collected around Sanford; only at this point, looking round, did they realise that the security droid was right behind them. They hid their reactions well – better than Sanford had – but he saw it in their faces.

Lurching a little, the train stopped. There was a cluster of people waiting to leave; a woman at the front pressed the button and the doors hissed open. Shuffling forward, Sanford heard a voice behind him:

'Excuse me, officer, I seem to have lost my way.'

As those ahead stepped gingerly and stiffly onto the platform, Sanford allowed himself another glance back. The man with the briefcase had got to his feet and planted himself between the revolutionaries and the droid: man and machine standing nose to nose.

'Excuse me, sir,' the android said blankly. Its voice was male and authoritative.

But the briefcase man was a law-abiding citizen and robots were programmed to be deferential to citizens.

'I'm looking for Oval Station,' the briefcase man said.

Sanford stepped out onto the platform.

'You require the Northern Line,' the android said.

The briefcase man laughed.

'And I'm on the Southern Line!' he said.

'That is correct.'

Ottoline stepped onto the platform.

'So how do I get to the Northern Line?'

The android explained as Krystan, then Glynis left the train.

'And how long does that take? I'm a bit late,' the briefcase man said.

The android gave him a time. Two teenagers stepped onto the train. The android tried to move forward and the briefcase man moved side to side confusedly in front of it. 'I'm sorry, I seem to be in the way.'

The train door closed. Sanford watched the android squeeze past the briefcase man, then the teenagers, to press the door control, but by then the train was moving. Sanford let out a deep breath and turned to the others.

'That was hairy,' said Ottoline.

'Was that man helping us?' Glynis said.

'I think so,' Sanford replied.

Relieved, a bit frightened, they moved on quickly. Shoving the pamphlet back in his rucksack, Sanford led them through an exit that took them to a pair of long escalators. They travelled up until they were back at ground level, then walked through the gates and out onto the street. They were at Matchett Station. This was a residential area and Penguin Station was only a ten minute walk away. Sanford suggested they head there, break the chain, and start again.

'Shouldn't we go quiet for a bit?' Krystan said. 'Maybe stop for the day?'

'Do you want to?' Sanford asked him. He looked at the others.

'Do you think that android reported us?' Glynis said.

'I doubt it. What's it going to report, it saw someone reading a pamphlet?'

'But it only takes a few minutes to share our images. They might be on the look out for us now.'

'I doubt it,' Sanford repeated, slightly irritably. 'It was just checking us out, I don't think it thought we were a big deal.' He didn't want to stop but he was trying hard to be democratic. 'They're not going to spend any more energy on it.'

'Cameras and robots take hundreds of images every day,' Ottoline added. 'I don't think we'll stand out.'

'Do you think we should carry on?' Krystan asked her.

'I think it would be okay to.'

'We'll just go to Penguin and break the circuit,' Sanford said. 'That'll be enough.'

Krystan looked at Glynis. Beyond their lives in the River of Life and hanging out with the Dream League, this trip was their first act of active resistance.

'Yeah?' he said.

'Okay then,' Glynis told him.

Sanford adjusted his rucksack and turned up the street.

'This way,' he said.

None of them had been to this part of town before. Penguin Station, when they reached it, was a neat little place with a single member of staff behind a booth and a flower stall just outside. A cramped elevator took them down to the platform, which was empty. A northbound train turned up almost immediately. On board, they wrote off Sanford's turn to drop a pamphlet as a bust, and moved on to Ottoline instead. They waited eight stops, right into London, changed at Brixton Station, left *The Truth About The Price* on Ottoline's seat, and headed straight south again.

On the next train they spotted a rival pamphlet. It had a glossy blue cover and was more professionally produced than Sanford's. On the front, above a simple design of a sunrise, was the title: *A Fair Price.*

Krystan picked it up.

'What's this?'

Sanford took it from him and flicked through its pages. He tutted.

'A Justice pamphlet.'

'Really?' Krystan took it back.

Sanford was dismissive. 'A Fair Price. It's just an unofficial Price based on dog eat dog.'

Glynis looked at him thoughtfully.

'What happened to Krystan would never have happened under their system.'

Sanford looked at his brother, and spoke more slowly than he had been about to.

'In theory. Not so much if you look at the history. All they're doing is replacing one Price with another.' He paused. 'You don't have to pay the Price at all. Nobody does.'

Glynis didn't push it. She didn't disagree – she just felt that she and Krystan might have avoided their fate in a system that was more… natural. Permeable.

Krystan waved the Justice pamphlet in the air.

'What shall I do with it?' he asked.

'In the spirit of democracy,' Sanford told him, 'put it back where you found it.'

They travelled for another hour, longer than they had planned to, up and down the Southern Line, with no more trouble from security droids, until they had passed most of the lunchtime rush and the trains were growing quiet again. Their shift was done. Standing on a platform once more, Sanford said:

'Head home?'

'Yes,' the other three said at once, tired.

It was a good day's work. They sat on a bench and waited for the train home, feet aching from traipsing from platform to platform. When the train came, they collapsed onto its seats without even thinking about pamphlets, and none emerged from Sanford's rucksack. But two stops from Turpin, Sanford suddenly remembered and pulled a copy from his rucksack. He read its first page, feeling pleased with it, and rested it against his lap. He looked at his brother and Glynis sitting opposite. He thought about the arguments between himself and Krystan, over the years, as Sanford had grown more rebellious, more intolerant. He looked at Ottoline, sitting beside him playing chess on her phone.

They pulled in at Turpin. Sanford nudged his sleepy brother with his foot.

'We're here,' he said.

They got to their feet and headed for the door. Remembering the pamphlet in his hand, Sanford dropped it onto a seat. Three people in the carriage – seated separately – looked up, looked at the pamphlet and looked at each other. As Sanford stepped out of the train, one of them picked it up and began to read.

4. DARCY

Four weeks after Krystan and Glynis's first ever pamphleteering trip, Darcy Herring called on her friend Shon who lived around the corner. It was early when Darcy left the house but Krystan, whose room she passed on the way out, was already up. In fact he had not yet reached his bed – his shift had just finished and he had popped home to pick up a couple of things before heading off to Glynis's place. His door was open and Darcy saw him packing his rucksack as she passed by in the hall.

'Good morning, Krystan!' she called brightly. She was thin, not very tall, and wearing a green and blue flowery dress she put on every spring.

Krystan looked up briefly, smiled wearily, and said quietly, 'Morning, Darcy.'

'Are you coming today?' she asked him.

'Yup.' He glanced at the window and the quiet street. 'You're a bit early.'

'Always early.' She adjusted the satchel that hung from her shoulder. 'I'm on placard duty with Shon.'

'I might see you later then,' Krystan said.

Darcy nodded.

'Or you might not. It's going to be a big crowd.'

She left the house, turned sharp left at the end of the street and stopped outside another house almost identical to her own. A woman roughly her own age and just as short but not as thin, with perfectly black hair, opened the door. She was wearing a dressing gown and looked sleepy.

'Morning!' Darcy said.

'Keep your voice down,' Shon told her. 'Everyone's asleep.'

Darcy frowned.

'You're not dressed,' she said.

'It's early.'

'They're expecting us at eight.'

'That's ages.'

Shon let her in and trudged upstairs to her room. The house was exactly the same layout as Darcy's, but a little newer, less frayed around the edges.

Shon made her bed so that Darcy could sit down.

'Have you eaten yet?' she asked.

Darcy patted her satchel.

'I've got a muffin for later.'

Shon grunted.

'I'm going to have a shower,' she said. She pointed to a small table that held a kettle, a glass jar and three mugs. 'Will you make me a coffee?'

'Sure.'

Shon disappeared. Darcy flicked the kettle on and

spooned instant coffee from the jar into two of the mugs. She sat on the bed and waited while the kettle rattled and steamed. There was a copy of a Justice pamphlet on the floor beside the bed, but Darcy couldn't be bothered to read it. When the kettle had boiled, she emptied it into the mugs and waited patiently until Shon returned, dressed and transformed but still grumpy.

She lunged for the coffee and sat beside Darcy.

'How come you're so full of the joys of spring,' Shon wanted to know.

'I feel good about today,' Darcy said. 'I think it's going to make a mark.'

Shon leaned back on one extended arm and took a sip.

'It's a permitted protest,' she said. 'And it's Justice.'

'It's better than nothing. And lots of others will be there, not just Justice people. We're going, for a start.'

'Hmm.'

'I think it's going to be big.'

'Hmm.'

'There's a momentum growing.'

'There does seem to be something,' Shon agreed.

She looked out the window. The sky was already blue. She looked at her coffee, half gone.

'Five minutes,' she said.

'Perfect,' said Darcy.

Darcy gazed around the room. Like her, Shon was a born payer and they had known each other for more than twenty years, after working together at a hospital in Gate. Darcy had introduced Shon to a resistance movement – the now defunct Shout – and although Shon had remained doggedly loyal ever since, it was Darcy who was the true believer, dragging a pessimistic but steadfast Shon alongside her. There was an old Shout poster on Shon's wall. Darcy had the same one at home.

They finished their coffee. Darcy adjusted the satchel strap on her shoulder.

'Right then,' she said. 'Let's go.'

*

They walked to a tall block of flats not far away and went round the back to a row of tatty garages. One of the garages was open and outside it stood a red van. Perched in the back of the van, his feet dangling, was a nervous looking young man neither Darcy nor Shon had met before. Standing near him was a serious young woman drinking a cola, who raised her head at them as they approached.

'Hey,' the young woman said.

'Hello Hiba,' Darcy said. She turned to the nervous lad. 'Who's this?'

'This is Ghayth, he's just joined us,' Hiba said. 'He's a friend of Krystan's,' she added.

Darcy raised her eyebrows.

'Is that so?'

'We work together,' said Ghayth.

'At Berets?'

'Yeah.'

'Nice to meet you, Ghayth.'

Ghayth smiled hesitantly and Darcy turned her attention back to Hiba.

'Where's Owen?'

'In the garage.'

Darcy and Shon walked around the van to the garage entrance. Inside, his hands on his hips, pondering a rackety collection of placards, was a beer-bellied, stubbled man in a cheap t-shirt and saggy jeans. He turned at the sound of their scuffling feet.

'Alright, Shon. Darcy,' he said.

They walked into the garage and stood beside him.

'Everything okay?' Darcy asked.

He nodded at the placards.

'They look a bit rubbish,' he said.

Shon and Darcy regarded the placards. They were a mixture of homemade efforts and identical printed signs – the latter carried simple slogans in black text on white card, two sheets stapled back to back atop crude wooden poles. There were three slogans to choose from: NOBODY NEEDS TO PAY; THE PRICE IS A LIE; EQUALITY IS NOT IMPOSSIBLE. They were plain, cheap and anonymous – and about two thirds of them were stained with patterns of grey or pale brown.

'Lee had a pile of these in his side car and drove into a ditch,' Owen complained. 'And the last time we used them, there was a hailstorm.'

Darcy laughed.

'They look alright. They're still in one piece,' Shon said.

'We'll look like amateurs next to Justice,' Owen said.

'We are amateurs,' Darcy told him, and Shon added, 'As long as you can read them, what does it matter?'

'I want people to take us seriously.'

'They'll take us seriously because we're payers out in force,' Darcy said. 'Not because our signs are fancy.'

'Having rubbish placards just shows we're the real deal,' said Shon.

Owen chuckled.

'You think Justice are going to drown us out,' Darcy told him.

'Yeah.'

'Lots of payers are in Justice,' she reminded him.

'I know.' He sighed.

Darcy put her hand on his arm.

'It's just one day. Let's piggyback on this and see what happens. If this was our demo, it wouldn't be allowed at all.'

Owen roused himself.

'You're right,' he said. He looked along the garage to the entrance.

'Hiba!' he called. 'Ghayth!'

As Ghayth and Hiba joined them, they each grabbed two or three placards and carried them a little awkwardly round to the back of the van. As they walked, Hiba demanded to know why the back of the van wasn't facing the garage entrance. 'I just reversed out and left it there,' Owen admitted. While the others waited, he climbed into the driver's seat and turned it around.

*

They drove into the centre of London – Owen and Hiba in the front, Darcy, Shon and Ghayth crouched in the back with heaps of placards and boxes of leaflets. There were even a few copies of Sanford's pamphlet, tied with an elastic band and sitting on top of a spare tyre. They drove mostly in silence. Darcy tried to make conversation with Ghayth, but he was monosyllabic and shy. The only time he became animated was when Darcy made a passing comment about the robots he worked with and he began explaining the different models in operation at the warehouse, until he saw the limit of her interest in her eyes and clammed up.

They stopped on a side road near Victoria Station. Once the placards were distributed, the van would wait here while they walked down Victoria Street to Parliament Square. The police – human and android – were already everywhere, watching. On the drive over they had been followed by four drones: one each, Hiba speculated, with Ghayth not having earned one yet. 'You'll have one after today,' she told him.

They parked the van and climbed out. About twenty people were waiting, mostly Leaguers, each with a drone – they huddled beneath a bespoke black cloud of surveillance, like a cartoon of perpetual gloom, covering them in shadow as they collected behind the van and Owen and Ghayth handed out placards.

Darcy and Shon took a placard each and stood waiting at the side. Owen and Hiba seemed to know most of those gathered here, but the person Owen spoke to most was an old, lanky man in an oversized grey jumper called Rollo. Rollo had tobacco stains on his fingers, a rare sight in this day and age, and deep, deep wrinkles. He seemed to find the day funny.

'These signs have seen better days mate,' he said.

Owen harrumphed. Rollo twiddled one in the air.

'Look at that dirty great stain. Oh well. I can get a better one from Justice in a bit.'

Owen glared at him and said:

'Have you seen them?'

'St James's Park, on my way here. They've got balloons.'

'Balloons?'

'Red balloons that say "Justice for All".'

'What's the point of bringing balloons?'

'How many have they got?' Darcy chimed in.

'I didn't see,' Rollo said, lowering his placard so the sign rested on the ground. 'A big bag. They had a machine and two youngsters inflating them.'

'Do you think they'll release them into the air?' Darcy wondered.

'I hadn't thought of that. I assumed they'd just dangle them above their heads.'

'The drones won't like that.'

'The drones'll shoot them down,' Rollo agreed. He held his fingers like a gun and pointed into the air. 'Pop! Pop! Pop!'

'Balloons,' Owen muttered. 'Were there many people?'

Rollo shook his head.

'Not many. It was early.'

He raised his placard again and twisted it a second time, examining it in the sunlight. Owen handed placards to the last few waiting and looked in on Ghayth inside the van.

'Plenty more?'

'Quite a few,' Ghayth responded.

Owen turned back to the street. New arrivals were ambling towards him; some had drones over their heads, some not. Across the road, the police continued to stare. Owen gazed back indifferently.

'Do you need us?' a voice said at his elbow – Darcy.

'What?'

'You three seem to have it covered,' Darcy said. 'Shon and I are going for a walk.'

'Alright. But come back and get some leaflets.'

'Okay!' Darcy said cheerfully.

She linked Shon's arm and they walked away.

'I want another coffee,' said Shon.

*

When they reappeared at just after nine, Owen was handing out bundles of leaflets to those willing to distribute them. He rolled his eyes as Darcy took a pack that she shoved straight into her bag where Shon was certain she would forget all about them.

'Right,' said Owen, slamming the van shut. 'Let's go.'

All those still hanging around the van moved off as one. Darcy and Shon picked up the placards Owen had saved for them and swung them upside down by their feet as they walked. Gazing around at the steady stream of demonstrators spread across Victoria Street and at the cars nudging cautiously past them, they wandered ahead in the flow and left Owen behind. Passersby regarded the protestors with amusement and nervousness, and Darcy and Shon returned their looks with smiles, wanting to be reassuring and enjoying the feeling of being a novelty. A homeless payer sitting in a shop doorway saluted. Shon saluted back.

At the end of the road, Parliament Square expanded out in front of them. The crowd was massive, much bigger than even Darcy had expected, filling the square and spreading well beyond its edges. A small stage stood flanked by two large speakers; a handful of people fussed around a microphone and Darcy heard a rumble of feedback or of something being connected. The sun was bright in the sky and it was a clear, perfect spring day. There were orange Justice placards everywhere, almost one to a person – JUSTICE FOR ALL; AN EQUAL CHANCE IN LIFE; TO EACH WHAT THEY HAVE EARNED – and the crowd was sprinkled with the red balloons Rollo had told them about. But in amongst them was a smattering of placards, some like Darcy's and Shon's, others homemade, that marked their carriers as agents of the League, or of Noise, or of the Werkers. There weren't many, but Owen's van load was about to double them.

Darcy raised her sign above her head and Shon followed suit. Darcy felt elated. Looking over the heads of the crowd, she watched the balloons bounce between placards or float on the ends of string. It was like a party, or a concert: much less intense, much less furtive or angry than the secret rallies and meetings she was used to. The comparison reminded her of something and she looked around the outskirts of the square. There they were – a single, motionless row of police androids, lining every road, circling the entire protest. Here, in the thick of the action, not a single human police was in sight. She looked up – there were the drones, buzzing overhead like midges, watching, recording.

Some of them were marked with red rectangles. Darcy nudged Shon's shoulder and pointed.

'Red drones,' she said.

At that moment, as though activated by Darcy's recognition, one of the red drones fired a single, sniper-like slice of laser straight into the heart of the crowd.

People screamed, shouted, scrambled clumsily away.

Another drone fired, twice.

Then another.

The crowd collapsed into panic, running in every direction, running into each other.

Darcy and Shon dropped their placards, grabbed each other's hands and ran as hard as they could back up Victoria Street. Those who had been behind them, those just joining the crowd, were already turning and fleeing.

Behind her Darcy heard more shots, more screams. She heard a voice, booming out from who knew where – a drone? An android? The speakers by the stage?

'THIS GATHERING IS PROHIBITED.'

The voice repeated its message again and again, on a loop, fading as they left it behind. When they could no longer hear the shots, they could still hear the voice; but when they could barely hear the voice, they could still hear the screams.

Their lungs hurt.

'I need to stop,' Shon pleaded, but Darcy kept her going. 'We need to reach the van,' she called between breaths. But Victoria Street was long and they couldn't keep running all the way. Quickly Darcy looked behind her and discovered that they were not being followed. Even the police around them in the street were only watching indifferently. She pulled her friend to the side, off the road and towards the shops that were locking their doors.

They stopped, bending double, breathing painfully.

Others ran or stumbled past them, some crying, some stunned, some shouting instructions or information to those ahead. A few stood in the middle of the road, watching the horror behind them. A young man yelled in rage at the police and then fled as an android began moving towards him. After less than a minute, still not recovered, Darcy said, 'Come on.'

They held each other's arms and walked, lungs working hard. The street seemed quieter – had it stopped, had the firing stopped? Darcy looked back, but from where she stood she couldn't see what was happening. They walked in silence and when they had nearly reached the van, they saw Owen running towards them.

'You two!' he said, relieved.

Darcy looked into his eyes.

'It was a trap,' she said simply.

5. GHAYTH

Five weeks after the attack on Parliament Square, Ghayth Bail had a call from his supervisor. Ghayth was climbing into the cabin of an automated forklift when his pager beeped a code 4: come to the office.

'Wait here,' he said to the android standing on the forklift's back step. 'I have to go and see Mr. Flynn.'

He walked across a vast warehouse echoing with the sounds of objects being dropped, dragged and lifted, to a set of metal steps leading to a long balcony. At the top, in one of a row of small offices overlooking the entire proceedings, he found Mr. Flynn sitting at his desk.

'You wanted to see me?' Ghayth said.

Mr. Flynn was a young man of Ghayth's own age. Ghayth happened to know that they were born within a month of each other. Mr. Flynn did not invite Ghayth to sit down. He pointed to a screen on his desk that Ghayth could not see.

'You were at the illegal demonstration,' he said.

'What?' Ghayth asked him dumbly.

'You were seen. I'm looking at a picture of you.'

Ghayth said nothing. He didn't know what to say, and in any case he was too scared to speak.

'You're lucky the government aren't pressing charges,' Mr. Flynn said.

Ghayth remained silent. He hadn't known the government weren't pressing charges; he hadn't heard anything since the day itself, apart from rumours, apart from news reports he didn't believe anyway.

'But Berets aren't happy,' Mr. Flynn went on. 'This is bad for the company name, staff breaking the law like that.' He tapped his keyboard and peered at his screen as though double-checking something. 'They're docking your wages by ten per cent for the next six months.'

'What?' Ghayth said again. It seemed to be all he was capable of saying.

'They're docking your wages by ten per cent for the next six months,' Mr. Flynn repeated patiently.

'I can't afford it,' Ghayth said, pointlessly.

'You should have thought of that.'

Ghayth looked at the young, neatly turned out man sitting in front of him. All he felt was his helplessness – there was no anger, no upset. Even the fear was quickly fading; in fact he was sinking into relief, that this might be the only penalty he faced. He stared at Mr. Flynn, entirely passively, in a way that his supervisor began to find unnerving. The young manager turned away and picked up a brown folder.

'There's a whole batch of mismatched tags from

yesterday,' he said, changing the subject. 'You're down as the shipper.'

Ghayth frowned.

'What time?' he asked.

'What time?' Mr. Flynn looked inside the folder. 'It was shipped out at 10.38am. The shipment had to be recalled.'

'Sorry.'

'I thought you were one of the better ones at record keeping.'

Again Ghayth was silent.

'It's coming back this evening,' Mr. Flynn went on. 'Open them up and put the tags right. Make sure you have a robot with you.'

'Okay.'

There was a pause. Ghayth continued to stand there. Mr. Flynn was about to dismiss him when he finally spoke.

'Will my wages be docked from this month or next month?' he said.

'What?' Mr. Flynn checked his screen. 'It doesn't say. I guess you'll find out soon enough.'

Ghayth opened his mouth to ask something more but Mr. Flynn interrupted him: 'You can go now,' he said.

Ghayth walked away, down to the warehouse and back to his forklift. He climbed into the cabin.

'Where to?' he said to the android, a thick-limbed, seven-feet model for heavy lifting.

'Bay 172,' the android told him.

*

Ghayth was working the nightshift. Other than his visit

to Mr. Flynn, the shift was uneventful. The mismatched delivery was returned at 9.42pm and Ghayth and a small data droid corrected the tags and repacked the boxes within an hour – the records were only mismatched by one column and it was easy to fix. It could have been done even more easily at destination. His shift ended at 6.30am and while others trudged to their lockers, Ghayth walked alone to an entrance covered by thick yellow rubber slats at the rear of the warehouse. He pushed through them into a short, wide corridor lined by two large doors on either side. He peered through the window of a door marked 'ROBOTS' and, seeing a face he recognised, pushed his way in.

Ryszard Tabor was standing at a large worktop holding a small device in one hand and tapping at it with a long, thin needle. He was one of three people in the room, all standing at worktops concentrating on a machine of some kind. One of them, a woman called Gazelle, was prodding at the eye in an android's head. The other, Jeffrey, close to retirement, had an entire android laid out in front of him and was busily applying a screwdriver to its knee. All three looked up when Ghayth entered. Gazelle and Jeffrey nodded. Ryszard, middle-aged with a warm smile, said, 'Ghayth! Shift over?'

'Yeah.'

'Good day?'

'Not bad.' He didn't mention Mr. Flynn and the docked wage.

'Look at this.'

Ryszard waved him over and showed him the device in his hand. It was a motion sensor, of the kind that every android had in multiple locations on their bodies, to detect movement from any direction whether within visual range or not. Ghayth inspected the crevice Ryszard had been scraping with his needle.

'How do you get grit in there, eh?' Ryszard chuckled. 'What's it been doing?'

'What kind of unit is it from?'

'Security droid. This sensor was lodged between its shoulder blades. All the thing does all day is stand in doorways. How did it manage to get all that muck in here?'

Ghayth laughed.

'I don't know.'

Ryszard handed him the sensor and the needle. As he did so, he looked briefly at a camera in the corner, but he knew that no one really cared enough to be paying attention.

'Here,' he said. 'You have a go. I'm getting frustrated with it. I don't know why they made them so hard to clean.'

'Can't you air blast it?'

'I tried. It didn't come off! But if you loosen it, we can try again. Then I can give you something more interesting to do.'

Ghayth poked and scraped at the stubbornly sticky grit while Ryszard wandered off to some crates lining the wall. Ghayth found it as tricky as Ryszard had, because he couldn't risk scratching the multiple lenses. But after a few minutes he succeeded in dislodging something, and whole flakes of whatever it was began disintegrating.

'I think I've done it,' he called out.

Ryszard returned.

'Really?' He took the sensor back and inspected it, closing one eye. 'Let's try it again then.'

They moved to a small air cleaner at the end of the worktop. 'You do the honours,' Ryszard said. Ghayth inserted the sensor and set the cleaner to a mild blast. Nothing. He raised the setting and tried again. Immaculate.

'Good as new,' Ryszard said. He crossed the room and handed the sensor to Jeffrey, still working on his prostrate android. Jeffrey waved a silent acknowledgement as Ryszard returned.

'Now,' Ryszard said. 'Something more worthy of your talents.'

He reached into a crate against the wall and heaved out a squat data droid, of the kind Ghayth had been working with on the mismatched tags, and laid it on the workbench.

'Now,' Ryszard said again. 'What are we going to do with this?'

*

They worked on it for a couple of hours. There were problems with its object recognition that were difficult at first even to identify, let alone fix, but between them they got there in the end. 'Ghayth,' Ryszard said when they were finished, 'in another life you would have been my supervisor.' Then, struck by the sadness of what he had said, he quickly clapped his young friend on the shoulder and said, 'By the way, I've got something for you.'

He turned to a small toolbox and returned with a large glass marble resting in his palm. A grey circle was etched into one side and from the opposite side protruded a silver disc and long lines of fibres.

Ghayth looked at his friend in delight.

'An A12 eyeball!' he said.

'It's a little scratched,' said Ryszard, pointing at the circle, 'but it's fully functional. It's not worth the expense of a repair and no one's going to miss it.'

He passed it to Ghayth, who squinted and turned it over in the light, like a jewellery dealer examining a diamond.

'Bahjat should be able to compensate for that,' he said, assessing the scratches.

'I'm sure he will,' Ryszard said.

Ghayth put the eye carefully into the inside pocket of his jacket.

'Thanks,' he said.

'You're welcome.'

'I'd better go.'

'Yes, you'd better. See you tomorrow.'

'See you tomorrow.'

With brief nods and waves to the others, Ghayth walked out of the lab and shuffled as invisibly as he could back to the warehouse and across to the main exit. Mr. Flynn was finished by now and wouldn't know he had loitered this late, but whichever supervisors were currently on duty might wonder (if they noticed or cared) why he was on site outside his shift. In fact, several supervisors knew full well the hours Ghayth spent in engineering and turned a benign blind eye. Some even considered that they got useful – if illegal – work from him. But there were a few, Mr. Flynn among them, who were vindictive enough to shut down this payer doing citizen work if they learned of it.

It was mid-morning and the sun was bright in the sky. Ghayth put on a baseball cap to shield his eyes. The walk home took an hour, from the industrial sector in Turpin through Turpin central and on into Gate. Above him hummed a single drone, something he had acquired since the attack on Parliament Square. It had appeared outside his front door the next morning and had been his constant companion since. When he told Hiba about it, she just said, 'You've graduated.' As he walked he kept his head down, seeing no one he knew and not wanting to, his mind mostly on the A12 eyeball and whether Bahjat's brain could compensate for it. Finally, the streets began to widen, the shops disappear, and a general increased disrepair seep into the roads and the buildings, as Turpin faded into Gate. Ghayth added about a quarter of an hour to his journey by avoiding the main roads and taking a zig-zag of side streets. But it didn't work:

'Ghayth!' said Officer Murray cheerfully.

He was on the other side of the street, stepping out of a block of flats, his round face scratched in a couple of places by his morning shave. An android emerged behind him, carrying a gun that it holstered as it stepped onto the pavement. Ghayth nodded quickly and kept walking.

'Hey, where are you going?' Officer Murray called sadly.

Ghayth kept moving.

'Wait!' Officer Murray snapped.

Ghayth stopped. He listened to the sound of the android's metal feet against the road and the shuffle of Officer Murray's jacket against his kit belt as they crossed towards him. But he did not turn to look at them.

'Where are you off to in such a hurry?' Officer Murray enquired.

'Just home.'

'Just home. Where have you been?'

'Work.' Officer Murray knew exactly where he had been.

'Night shift, is it?'

'Yes.'

'Are you talking to the wall?'

Ghayth turned to face him.

'Seen any of your friends lately?' Officer Murray asked him.

'What friends?'

'What friends. Your friends from Parliament Square.'

'No,' Ghayth lied.

'Not even Hiba?'

'What?'

'Not even your friend Hiba?'

'No.'

Officer Murray's right hand shot out and shoved into Ghayth's left shoulder, pushing him against the wall. Ghayth's head knocked into the brickwork but not hard. The android took a single step forward.

'Are you lying to me, Ghayth?'

'No,' said Ghayth, slightly whiningly, looking down.

'You've been friends with Hiba for a long time,' Officer Murray said. 'She's practically family. But you haven't seen her for five weeks? After a traumatic event like that?'

'We don't see each other that often,' Ghayth said. 'I'm usually at work.'

Officer Murray released Ghayth's shoulder.

'You do work long hours,' he agreed. He pointed to the drone above them. 'So if I were to call down data from your drone here, it would report no evidence of you meeting Hiba, or any of the others.'

'No,' Ghayth repeated. It was a pointless lie in one way – Officer Murray would already have any data the drone held, he already knew Ghayth was lying. But denial was the only defence Ghayth had – not to prevent Officer Murray from knowing, but to ward off more questions, to keep this interaction as short as possible.

Officer Murray lifted the baseball cap from Ghayth's head and examined it. It was work-issue, with the Berets logo across the front.

'I think you're full of it,' the officer said. 'You get these for free?'

'No, we have to pay for them.'

Officer Murray turned it over in his hand, glanced briefly at the android, and dropped it on the ground.

'See you tomorrow, Ghayth,' he said.

*

Reaching home, Ghayth didn't feel like eating. He fetched himself a glass of water and went to his room. He was getting used to these encounters with Officer Murray and their effect was waning, but that was the first time the officer had shoved him like that. It felt as though the more Ghayth grew used to it, the more it escalated. Ghayth wondered how much Officer Murray's android partner would tolerate, and how far Officer Murray would go.

He hung his jacket on the back of the door and retrieved

the A12 eyeball. His bed lined one side of the narrow room and a low wooden bench lined the other. The bench was like a miniature replica of Ryszard's worktop in the engineering lab. It was littered with small pieces of equipment, most of it unidentifiable to the non-roboticist eye. Ghayth knelt in front of the bench and placed the A12 eyeball carefully before him. He reached beneath the bench and pulled out a small tin toolbox. He reached beneath the bench a second time and pulled out a second tin box. This second box needed a code to open. From inside he lifted a cube of metal, about the height of two thick books lying flat, with a single cylinder protruding from its top and spindly arms ending in pincers jutting from either side. On its back was a tiny keypad, its keys so small Ghayth had to press them with a pin. As he did so, a row of lights across the cube's front switched on, red then amber then green.

'Activated,' said a quiet, young, male voice.

'Hello, Bahjat,' Ghayth said.

'Hello Ghayth,' said Bahjat. It paused, then added: 'It is morning. Have you completed your shift?'

'Yeah.'

'Was it a good day?'

Ghayth shrugged. He didn't want to talk about Mr. Flynn's salary penalty or Officer Murray's persecution.

'I've had worse.'

'Did you visit the lab?'

'Of course – I've got some exciting news!'

'What is that?'

Ghayth held up the A12 eyeball, even though he knew that all that Bahjat could detect was the movement of his hand and the infrared of his body heat.

'Ryszard gave me an A12 optic!'

'Excellent,' Bahjat said. 'Is it fully operational?'

'I think so. It's got some scratches so there may be distortion to compensate for, but not much. I think you can handle it.'

'Excellent,' Bahjat repeated.

'I'm going to install it now,' Ghayth told him. 'So I'll have to close down again for a bit.'

'Understood.'

Ghayth entered a second code into Bahjat's back. The lights passed through a reverse sequence – green, amber, red – and went out. Ghayth reached into his toolbox, selected half a dozen instruments, and set to work.

His first act was to loosen and remove the cylinder from Bahjat's top, detach several wires that hung from its base, and set it to one side. His second was to remove the lid of the cube body to reveal an elaborate orchestra of electronics inside. After that his task was to attach the A12 eyeball to the top of the cylinder and feed its spray of fibres through the cylinder itself, connecting them carefully to the operations within the cube.

It was a complicated and fine-tuned job that would take a few hours of patient and careful work. Ghayth had built Bahjat himself, over years, with pieces of equipment and tools given him by Ryszard and others. The result – the web of electronics and positronics inside the cube – was impressively harmonious and systematic, given the hodge-podge nature of his materials. Bahjat was an almost fully sentient (in robot terms) data-processing droid with a sophistication matching that of his professionally constructed counterparts. Once, a year ago, Ryszard had discretely visited Ghayth at home to see Bahjat for himself. He had been amazed. And that had been an earlier version – Ghayth had made a lot of progress since.

He worked in silence, contentedly, hoping to complete the task before he needed to sleep and ignoring his growing hunger, though he knew that eventually he would have to break to eat. But as his mind started wandering repeatedly towards food, there was a tap at his door. He paused, holding his torch and the A12 eyeball in mid-air in front of him.

'Who is it?' he called.

'It's me,' said Hiba.

'It's open.'

Ghayth's room was usually bolted shut from the inside but today he had forgotten to lock it. Hiba pushed her way in holding aloft a carrier bag.

'Chips!' she said.

Ghayth smiled and put the eyeball on the worktop.

'What's that?' Hiba asked him, moving to the bed and pulling two bundles of warm paper from the bag.

'An A12 eyeball.'

'From Ryszard?'

'Yeah.'

Hiba looked at her friend questioningly.

'Is it a big deal?'

'They're hard to get hold of.'

He sat next to her on the bed and took one of the bags of chips, opening it on his lap.

'Thanks,' he said.

Hiba sighed.

'I gained another drone this morning.'

'Another one?'

'That's five now. What do they need with five for one person? I swear they have more drones than they know what to do with.'

'Government intelligence is a mess.'

'Hmm. Sanford Hoad says that government incompetence is the only thing keeping us all out of prison.'

'Or internal sabotage.'

Hiba paused with a fat chip in mid-air.

'What?'

'I think there are people inside government deliberately messing things up.'

'Why do you think that?'

Ghayth shrugged.

'It would explain a lot.' He ate a few mouthfuls quickly, suddenly very hungry. 'But you're alright? No trouble?'

Hiba shook her head.

'I'm fine. Nothing.'

After the attack on Parliament Square they had expected a clampdown – extra androids roaming the streets, red drones, curfews, arrests, raids. But apart from an increase in drone surveillance and a few individuals receiving punishments from their workplaces, there had been no change. Everyone went about their business as before, the general population seemed to accept that the protest had always been illegal, and the government's main activity seemed to be merely condemning the demonstrators in press releases, mostly directed at Justice. Why the government had allowed the protest and then attacked it, nobody knew. It was confusing, and unnerving.

'But what about you, robot boy? Still not looking after yourself I see.'

Ghayth looked around his perfectly clean and tidy room.

'I'm alright.'

'When would you have fed yourself if I hadn't shown up?'

'I would have eventually.'

'After spending five hours hunched over your new eyeball.'

Ghayth had no reply.

'But you're okay?' Hiba pressed him.

'I'm alright,' he repeated. 'But Berets have docked my wages.'

'Because of the square?'

'That's what they said.'

'How much?'

'Ten per cent for the next six months.'

'That's steep.'

'There's been worse.'

'We'll talk to the River,' Hiba said firmly. 'See if they can help. Are you coming tomorrow?'

'Yes,' he said, but without conviction.

'You should.'

'I will.'

'When was the last time you went out anywhere?'

Ghayth cast his mind back.

'I'm not sure.'

'You need to see people, Ghayth. It's not good for you being in here so much.'

'I see people at work.'

'It's not the same. You need your friends.'

'Ryszard is my friend.'

'I know he is. But he's like a… he's more like a kindly schoolteacher. And he's not a payer. You need friends who live in the same world as you.'

'I know,' he conceded.

'So you'll come.'

'Who'll be there?'

'The usual. Owen. Imelda. Meirong. Krystan. Ottoline.'

'Okay.'

'Good.'

They ate in silence for a little while. Then Ghayth said:

'I saw Officer Murray again today.'

'Where?'

'On the way home this morning.'

'What did he say?'

'He asked if I'd seen anyone from Parliament Square again. He asked if I'd seen you.'

Hiba tutted contemptuously.

'He shoved me against the wall,' Ghayth added.

Hiba had been about to dip a chip into ketchup, but instead she dropped it back onto the paper.

'He shoved you into a wall?'

'Yeah.'

'Was there an android there?'

'Yeah.'

'What did it do?'

'Nothing. It took a step forward like it was about to step in, but he only pushed me once so I guess it didn't think it needed to.'

'What happened after that?'

'Nothing. He went off after a minute.'

'Are you okay?'

'I'm scared of him,' Ghayth said simply.

Hiba looked at him for a long moment and put her hand on his forearm.

'He can't hurt you,' she said. 'Not in front of the android. He's got no cause.'

Suddenly Ghayth's voice was deeper, a sob bubbling beneath it. 'But after the square... how much will the android tolerate when it's a payer, not a citizen? What if he finds me on his own?'

Hiba squeezed his forearm a little tighter, as though pressing home her point.

'He can't patrol on his own,' she said. 'Forget about the square, that was different. You're the robot boy, you know there are laws about these things. If the citizens found out a robot let a dodgy cop hurt someone, they would freak. It would be... it would be disorderly, wouldn't it.'

Ghayth took a deep breath.

'You're right,' he said. He straightened his back. 'It's messed up. They'll watch androids shoot down a hundred people and not bat an eyelid, but one beating outside the rules and everyone's outraged.'

Hiba reached into her carrier bag and pulled out two colas, handing one over.

'That's citizens for you,' she said.

*

Hiba stayed for another hour, chatting about lighter things, and then left Ghayth to his new eyeball. He got back to work, and in a little over three hours the eye was installed and the software updated. He switched Bahjat back on.

'Activated,' Bahjat said.

'Notice anything different?' Ghayth asked him.

There was silence.

'Configuring,' Bahjat said eventually.

More silence.

'I have visual,' Bahjat announced.

'It's worked! Can you see me?'

'I can see you, Ghayth.'

'Full colour?'

'Full colour.'

'What about the scratches?'

'Compensating.'

'You mean you're still compensating?'

'Yes. Compensation complete in twenty two seconds.'

They waited in silence for twenty two seconds.

'Compensation complete.'

'So what's it like?'

'My systems are using data from unimpaired sensory inputs to correct for impaired sensory inputs. I do not perceive the impaired data unless I choose to.'

'What's it like?'

'It is visual.'

Ghayth hesitated. Of course he knew that Bahjat would not feel anything, but still he wanted some kind of reaction.

And his work on Bahjat so far was impressive enough that Bahjat realised this.

'The range and scope of my sensory data and options is greatly increased,' he said. 'My capacity for interaction with my environment is greatly enhanced. It is… liberating.'

*

Ghayth eventually disciplined himself to get some sleep, but not until the evening – and by 11.00 that night he was up again and walking out the front door, heading back to Berets and the shift starting at midnight.

It was very dark outside. This part of Gate was badly lit, and what lights there were often flickered or cut in and out. Ghayth kept his head down and walked quickly and purposefully. It was no good taking the side streets at this time of night – too dangerous – so he stuck to the main roads and walked their wider and more populated pavements. But here, there were more police.

He wasn't wearing his baseball cap anymore, he was looking at the ground, and he was wearing dark clothes – but still Officer Murray spotted him. The officer was leaning under a streetlamp narrowly watching a group of teenagers huddled in front of a chippy. The teenagers were nervously talking amongst themselves, throwing occasional glances the policeman's way. The android stood to attention beside its partner, apparently staring at nothing. Ghayth saw Officer Murray first and kept walking, hoping the kids were occupying the cops' attention and that he could slip by unnoticed. But no.

'Ghayth,' Officer Murray said in a low voice.

Ghayth didn't try to pretend he hadn't heard. He stopped and turned.

'Off to work?' Officer Murray asked him.

'Yes.'

'Seen your friends today?'

Ghayth was tired. He hadn't allowed himself enough sleep.

'You already know,' he said.

'What?'

Ghayth looked at the drone above his head.

'You know where I've been, you don't need to ask me.'

Officer Murray raised himself from the streetlamp and walked closer to the young warehouse worker.

'Ghayth,' he said. 'Watch your attitude.'

Ghayth rubbed his hand across his eyes and said nothing.

'Have you seen your friends today?' Officer Murray repeated.

'No.'

'Don't lie to me, Ghayth.'

Ghayth sighed. He found that he was out of patience, and somehow too tired to feel too frightened. Was Murray going to force him to report on his friends even when the police already knew all his movements, just for the sake of making him say it? What was the point? But Murray didn't care about that. It was just a line.

'Don't lie to me, Ghayth,' the officer said again.

'I haven't seen anyone.'

Officer Murray reached for his belt and Ghayth flinched. But he was just checking a reading or something, some information being sent by his office.

'Jumpy,' Officer Murray said.

They looked at each other. For possibly the first time, Ghayth stared directly into Officer Murray's eyes, at the contempt and the gloating and the arrogance. At the violence.

Ghayth turned away and spoke to the android.

'You're not supposed to allow harm to humans,' he told it.

'You're not a citizen,' Officer Murray interjected.

Ghayth ignored him.

'You're not supposed to allow harm to humans except in the enforcement of the law,' he said to the android, quoting almost verbatim from the Security Unit Programming Explanatory Manual. 'Even payers,' he added.

'I am enforcing the law,' said Officer Murray, irritated.

'This isn't enforcement of the law,' Ghayth said to the android. 'Officer Murray already has the information he needs and I'm not under interrogation.'

Ghayth passed from weary to a new adrenalin rush. He wasn't sure what he was doing, but appealing to the robot, that he understood and could handle so much more easily than people, seemed like a way out. Or at least a way around. But it could just as easily be his undoing.

The android turned its heavy head and the lights on its face bore down on Ghayth.

'He is not harming you,' it said.

'He's causing psychological harm,' Ghayth replied without skipping a beat.

'Psychological harm is outside my parameters.'

Ghayth thought quickly.

'You are making harm more likely,' he said after a pause. 'You are… allowing a harmful situation… you're allowing a situation… behaviour… that is likely to result in harm. You are… creating the conditions for harm.' He was thinking aloud. 'It is the early stages of harm. You are not applying policy strictly enough. You are not complying with your protocols correctly. Or sufficiently.'

He stopped, hoping one of these phrases had cut through. The android was silent.

'What are you playing at?' Officer Murray snapped.

Ghayth and the policeman looked at the unmoving android.

'What's wrong?' Officer Murray asked it.

'I must consider,' the robot said.

They waited. Officer Murray cast Ghayth a furious look but said nothing. Finally, the android announced:

'We must let this individual pass. This interaction breaches policy.'

'You're kidding,' said Officer Murray.

'No,' the android told him.

'I'm just asking him questions,' the policeman insisted.

'That is inaccurate,' the android said. Then it added, to Ghayth's surprise: 'In the context of previous interactions with this individual.'

Officer Murray gave the android a disgusted look. Then he turned squarely to Ghayth.

'Nice move,' he said. 'You know all I have to do is ask for a different unit next patrol? This trick won't work twice.'

Ghayth was still looking at the android, not quite believing what he had done.

'Say hello to your friends,' Officer Murray said threateningly and walked away. The android followed.

Ghayth watched them go. Behind him, the teenagers outside the chippy cheered.

6. WALID

Six weeks after Ghayth installed Bahjat's A12 eyeball, Walid Rawlins made a phone call to a fake number connecting him to a computer. The computer responded with a standard automated 'please leave a message' audio, and Walid obediently left a message.

'It's me. I'm running a little later than expected, I'll be there in half an hour. Mine's a whisky.'

He hung up. He had made the call from a landline in his office, for the benefit of anyone snooping. Now he walked from his office to the shop floor and made his way to the front of the bookstore where Ottoline was sitting at the counter.

The shop was quiet and Ottoline was reading a book. It was after 9.00 in the evening and still light outside, a warm July night. But still Ottoline wore the motorcycle jacket that she was never without.

'I'm heading out now,' Walid told her. 'Are you okay

to close up tonight?' He liked to keep the store open until 10.00.

'Sure,' she told him.

'Who's here with you?' he asked, forgetting his own rota.

'Glynis is shutting up the café, she'll be up here in a minute.'

'Okay, good. Goodnight, Ottoline.'

'See you tomorrow, Mr. Rawlins,' Ottoline smiled.

He picked up a couple of bills that were lying on a shelf behind the counter and returned to his office. Dropping the bills on his desk, switching off the lights, he locked the office behind him and crossed the back of the store to a small side exit. Outside was a wide side street occupied by stacks of flattened cardboard boxes and two large, heavy-lidded bins. Three drones were waiting for him. He took a good look at them, let them have a good look at him. He had acquired one extra drone since the Parliament Square bloodshed, only one. Others had found their drones doubling and more. There were rumours that a pamphleteer in Peckham now had ten.

He walked along the side street and turned a corner to the front of the store, where he saw Ottoline still reading uninterrupted at the counter. He walked down Turpin High Street and turned right, crossing the road and heading down Cormorant Lane. The further he went, twisting and turning along the way, the quieter the streets became – but his journey ended in a pub, The Almond and Ball, named after the law firm that occupied the building before the wars, squeezed between two narrow houses. Two dozen drones fluttered outside it. His own three joined them and he stepped inside.

The pub was dark and sounded only of murmuring voices and the clack of a pool table at the back. Everyone inside was Walid's age – he was nearing sixty – or older, sitting around small tables and talking quietly. A few turned at Walid's entrance and some nodded in acknowledgement. Walid went straight to the bar, where a very tall woman with a beehive hairdo that made her into a giant was pouring two whiskies.

'Belinda, evening,' Walid said.

'Walid,' she said warily. She took the whisky drinker's money and filed it in the till. 'Passing through?'

'In a while.' He glanced towards the window, at the sky still dark blue. 'At nightfall.'

'Usual, then?'

'Please.'

She poured him a bourbon of his own.

'Zian here?' Walid asked as he hugged the glass towards him.

Belinda nodded and moved to another customer at the far end of the bar.

Walid drank his bourbon in silence. By the time he was finished it was dark outside. He placed his glass firmly on the counter and walked to the back of the pub, passing through a door that led to the kitchen and turning sharp right into another room. Zian's office.

Zian was nowhere to be seen. Walid knelt in a corner behind Zian's small wooden desk and pulled up a floorboard. From beneath it he retrieved a long cardboard box. Locking the office door by tapping a keypad, Walid proceeded to quickly undress. He removed his soft green shirt, black vest, smart black trousers and brogues, draping his clothes over the back of a chair. From the cardboard box he unfolded a different costume: a dark grey shirt, a thin black jacket, black jeans and boots. He put this outfit on and packed his former clothes into the same box. From inside one of the new jacket's pockets he pulled a small, circular container holding two contact lenses that lightened the colour of his eyes and altered the pattern of his irises. Inside the box he found two more items: a wig that lengthened his hair a little and returned it to the consistent black of his youth and a grey Berets baseball cap. He didn't like wigs, he felt silly wearing them, but it was effective. The final touch was a pair of round, wire-rimmed glasses tucked into another of the jacket's pockets.

Transformed from one plainly dressed nobody to another – but another with no history of association with seditious groups and no drones assigned to him – he returned the cardboard box to its nook in the floor and replaced the floorboard. Leaving Zian's office, he once again bypassed the kitchen and took a steep flight of steps down to a damp and unlit cellar. Lighting his way with his phone, he passed an unruly stack of crates and barrels to a locked door. He entered a code and passed through it into a long, thin, concrete corridor that stretched both left and right as far as he could see. In fact it ran beneath the entire street and into the street beyond. It was lit by flickering and buzzing lamps clumsily rigged along the ceiling and it was lined with locked doors. Walid turned right and walked unhurriedly but purposefully, heading beyond Crown Street above him towards an exit point beneath Varda Road. Ahead, two figures emerged quietly from a cellar door, locked it carefully behind them (with both a keypad and a physical key) and began moving in his direction. They were two women, one in a smart business suit and carrying a briefcase, the other in jeans and a t-shirt. The one in the suit watched Walid suspiciously as they approached; the one in jeans did not seem to expect to recognise anyone. As they grew closer, the suit scrutinised his face more and more narrowly. Walid removed his glasses and cap to make her life easier. When they were about a metre distant, her face suddenly softened.

'Walid,' she said, relief in her voice.

'Good evening, Esta,' he smiled.

The corridor was too narrow for them to pass each other easily. Walid moved closer to the wall and turned at an angle to make way. Esta smiled in return; jeans looked a little nervous.

'Out and about again,' Esta observed.

'The revolution won't run itself,' he said.

Esta chuckled at that and the two parties went on their way. Esta was not part of the resistance and did not particularly believe in it – did not particularly care whether the country was run by the PON, the Dream League or a circus master, as long as whoever was in charge left her alone. This long underground corridor, and others like it, was not constructed by the political groups Walid associated with. It was carved by the criminal organisations that had controlled Turpin during the Brutalisation and were still prominent now, in an uneasy accommodation with the River of Life and the other villages that had grown up when government suppression relaxed. The corridors provided a patchy but effective hidden network through Turpin and Gate, allowing the discrete movement of goods and people away from the eyes and recording devices of drones, androids and police. As far as anyone knew, the government was oblivious to the tunnels' existence. Some of the Turpin corridors belonged to the Cloud Gang, the rest were shared between the Hooper and Stanhold families. The corridors in Gate were controlled by either the Vanes, the MacMartins or the Daubers. This particular corridor was controlled by the Hoopers and managed by Milla Hooper, Esta's older sister. Certain individuals in the resistance movements – individuals in the leadership and key operatives, Walid among them – were granted free use of the tunnels: partly because some in the families shared the resistance's goals, partly because they shared an interest in subverting the surveillance system. And of course deals were done. The revolutionaries had networks that were useful to smugglers and thieves. The revolution was not pure.

Walid's own roots were in the Hoopers. He had come to the River of Life in his middle years and had joined it discretely, subtly. Few in the League or the River were sure what role he played, if they knew he played a role at all. He saw himself as a connector. He knew a lot of people and he had resources. He made things happen, but he did not do those things himself.

He was almost at the end of the corridor when he stopped by a tatty blue door and entered yet another code. With his way of life, it was a good job he had a head for numbers. The door clicked open and he slipped inside. This cellar was very different to the Almond and Ball's – glaringly bright, filled with ordered rows of wide racking stacked with fridges, microwaves, vacuum cleaners. Standing sentry by a second door at the other end of the cellar was a basic, dormant warehouse droid with caterpillar tracks rather than legs. Walid passed through that door and up a flight of clean steps into a spacious, pristine branch of PLUTO, quite possibly the fanciest shop in Turpin. This branch, like the corridors below it, was run by a Hooper. The store was still open. Walid hovered at the back, loitering by a row of washing machines. A jumpy young man in a white shirt scuttled over to him. The PLUTO name badge on his chest said *Callum: Assistant Manager*.

'Good evening, sir,' he said nervously.

'Good evening, Callum,' Walid said.

'What can I help you with?'

'An exit.'

Callum surveyed the store. He nodded.

'That family,' he said, his forehead indicating a couple and two teenagers by a display of turntables, talking to a sales assistant, 'have just bought a record player and are arranging home delivery. They'll be leaving any minute.'

'Thank you, Callum.'

Walid wandered to the same corner and toyed with a CD player. By chance it was the exact same player as the one in his office. After a short time he heard the family saying goodbye. He turned and left the store right behind them, as though he was with them. Helpfully a young woman tumbled into the store at the same moment. Walid hovered behind the family for about twenty metres down the street before peeling himself away and walking in the opposite direction.

No drone followed him. No drone knew who he was. And none seemed to have been alerted by this man leaving a shop he never entered. PLUTO was at the nice end of Turpin – the citizen end – where the drones were less numerous and less observant. Walid walked towards Turpin Station and, as he neared, the drones in the air above grew thicker, but not by much. At this point his journey had been an almost perfect loop – the bookstore was only a short walk away.

He passed through the station's gates with a pay-as-you-go and on the escalators he slipped on a health mask – one extra layer of disguise for a while. He looked downwards and kept his face from the cameras as much as he could without looking odd. He caught a northbound train and jumped off at the first stop, Dabiri.

Leaving the station, he turned a sharp right into Grenville Street and walked for ten minutes until he reached a car park occupied mostly by vans and small trucks – a holding park for businesses. He crossed to a yellow transit van with large YOURDOORNOW logos on either side. He reached underneath the van on the passenger side, scrabbled around and eventually retrieved a key. He opened the van and settled in behind the wheel. On the passenger seat was a thin yellow YOURDOORNOW tabard. He wriggled into it and started the engine.

Walid didn't drive very often these days but he liked it, especially at night. He liked the faint hum of the electrical engine and the soothing ticks of the indicator light, and he liked navigating the roads in the warm and the dark. In his youth he had driven for the Hoopers, but those drives had been brief and frantic. He was a calmer man now.

He drove for a quarter of an hour, a direct route along the main roads from Turpin to Lethbridge. Anything indirect might have looked odd to the cameras (who knew which details they picked up on and which they missed?). He drove to a block of flats – in fact to two blocks of flats that shared a wide underground car park. He took the van through the entrance for the east block and parked it between a large black 4x4 and the wall. Stepping out, he walked round to the back of the van, climbed inside and emerged momentarily with a cardboard box hugged in his arms. He locked the van behind him and walked across the dim car park to the elevator for the west block. He pressed the button for the second floor.

The lift took him to a warm, lavender-walled corridor that he followed to a grey door marked B4. He knocked. He waited. Presently the grey door opened to a woman close to Walid's own age with a severe crewcut and dressed in black. She stepped aside and indicated with a sweep of her arm that he should bring the box inside. He did as she asked. As he lowered the box to the ground in the long hallway, she closed the door behind them.

'Good journey?' she asked him.

'All clear, as far as I could tell,' he said, turning from the box to face her.

They shared a brief hug.

'What's in the box?' She smiled.

'I've no idea, but it's heavy,' he complained.

They opened it to see. It was a set of saucepans. They laughed.

'What would have been wrong with towels?' he asked plaintively.

'Come on in,' she said.

She led him to a large kitchen with a rustic-looking

wooden table in its centre. Walid sat down. His host hovered by the work surface.

'Do you want something to drink?' she said.

'Tea is fine.'

She put the kettle on and leaned where she stood.

'How have you been, Ravi?' he asked her.

She shrugged.

'Unnerved,' she said. 'Nothing has changed.'

'Nothing?'

'Not for me. It seems they already have me where they want me.'

'There's a lot they don't know,' he said optimistically.

'That's true. But I haven't even had my drones go up.'

'You haven't?'

'Have you?'

'Only by one.'

'Well, that's something. There's a guy in Peckham who now has ten, apparently.'

'My employees have all acquired a couple of extra each. That seems to be where their interest lies. Or where their information leads them.'

'They've come down on Justice very hard. They don't know what's hit them.'

'Is that right?'

'There have been arrests.'

Walid raised his eyebrows, surprised.

'A handful of medium-level people,' Ravi went on. 'The PON's line is that irresponsible elements have infiltrated Justice's organisation and led it to make unwise choices. But the top and the bottom of Justice are just being watched.'

'I wonder what they're up to.'

'I think,' Ravi said, 'they don't know what they're doing.'

By now the kettle had boiled. Ravi set about making the tea.

'Really?' Walid asked her.

Ravi nodded as she poured.

'They're freaking out about something but they don't know what to do about it.'

She put a spoon in the sink.

'That makes them liable to lash out,' Walid said.

'Like they did.'

She put a mug of tea in front of him.

'Shall we go to the front room?'

Walking through, Ravi sat in an armchair – her armchair, the one she always used – while Walid took the sofa at a forty-five degree angle from her.

'It's been almost three months since Parliament Square,' Ravi said. 'Drone activity has increased almost everywhere. Targeted at our groups but also general surveillance of both payers and citizens. But it's just surveillance. We don't know if there's been any increase in bugging, we haven't found any evidence of it yet, but they're good at hiding it. There's been no increase in red drones and none in androids. They're just watching.'

She paused before moving on, to ask:

'I guess that fits with what you've seen?'

Walid nodded and sipped his tea.

'Like I said, only one extra drone for me. But my employees at the store... Glynis now has four. Ottoline has six, Milya has two. Even Dana has two and she's not

involved in anything. And the Leaguers who use the store...
it's gone up across Turpin, as you say. Everything I hear is
as you describe. There's no increase in harassment, only in
drones. Nobody is finding extra bugs in their rooms. No
attempt to restrict movement or limit meetings. They just
seem to want us to know they're watching.'

'Unless you're Justice. The last figure I heard for the
arrests was seven. All of them still in jail.'

'What charge?'

'Disorder. And the PON have removed Justice's access
to media. They're as limited now as the League – they're
reduced to pamphlets and posters. Some of their accounts
have been frozen too. They've even come to us asking for
help moving money.'

'What do you think's driving it? They can't believe
Justice are a threat.'

'We think the PON believe that Justice are the biggest
potential catalyst for a mass movement. They don't take us
very seriously and also believe they have us under control.
But whatever it is that's upset them, it's made them turn
on Justice.'

'Can they really think Justice are the seeds of
revolution?'

'You don't see them up close as I do, Walid. Some of
them can barely tell Justice and the others apart. They
think the main difference is that one is professional and
the other is full of cranks. Yes, I think they see Justice as
an extreme threat – I mean, they do now. They started to
recently. We just don't know why.'

Walid took some more tea.

'Something has made them suspect that we have

people close to the centre,' Ravi went on. 'So – a show of force against the mainstream mass movement in Parliament Square, a clampdown on the only legitimised anti-Price organisation, and a big show of watchful eyes over the rest of us. To intimidate whatever it is they think they've detected, suppress support for it.'

Ravi put her tea on a little table beside her chair. 'Well – there you have it. That's our update, such as it is. Short on detail, I'm afraid.'

'As expected, under the circumstances. All sides watching and waiting.' Walid crossed his ankles and rested his mug on his knees, relaxing a little. 'I have a couple of items of local business.'

Ravi waited.

'The River of Life have formed a union in Gate,' Walid told her.

'In Gate!'

'That's right.'

Ravi was delighted.

'Why am I only hearing about this now?'

'It's been extremely slow and cautious,' he told her. 'I only know the vaguest details, no one has taken me much into their confidence. It doesn't have the sympathy in management that the Turpin unions have. But it has members and resources. It has strength.'

'That's a big step.'

'It's a big shift,' Walid agreed. 'They may need money,' he added. 'At the moment they depend on the Turpin River, but that's not sustainable for long.'

'We'll do what we can,' Ravi said. 'Let them know they have friends at this end.'

Walid nodded.

'A union in Gate,' Ravi said, smiling.

'One more thing, a small thing,' Walid went on.

'Yes?'

'A few weeks ago I made some enquiries with Ahdaf about a policeman in Gate called Cliff Murray...'

'Oh yes, I know about that.'

'... who has been persecuting a payer and League member called Ghayth Bail.'

'Yes. Yes. How did this come to you?'

'His League friends brought it to me, asking for a favour. It wasn't a problem the union or the River could deal with in the normal way.'

'No.'

'I haven't heard anything for a while. I'm told by Ghayth's friends that Officer Murray has gone, however.'

'Yes. It was done very quickly. Officer Murray was assigned to desk duty down south somewhere. He was given twenty-four hours notice, shoved into official accommodation and put on report.'

Walid chuckled.

'Was that you?'

Ravi smiled.

'I spoke to Bill. He was quite annoyed about it. He knocked some heads together and there was some good drone footage of the officer's behaviour.'

'Good old drones.'

'Love 'em.'

'These little victories, they keep us going, don't they.'

Walid put his mug on the coffee table and got to his feet.

'I'd better go, Ravi. This is quite long enough for a delivery driver to hang around for.'

'People will wonder what we've been doing.'

They walked to the hallway and hugged again.

'Thank you for the saucepans,' Ravi said.

'You're welcome. Enjoy.'

'Be careful. I don't know how we'll talk next time. Someone will be in touch.'

'I understand. It's an uncertain time.'

Walid paused with his hand on the door.

'Be careful yourself, Ravi,' he said.

'Don't worry.'

Walid passed through the door and Ravi closed it behind him. He called the elevator, beginning a rewind of his journey – from van to tube to electronics store to pub to bookstore via one abandoned disguise – back to his life, and to waiting for whatever was coming.

7. RAVI

Seven weeks after her visit from Walid, Ravinder Babbington's phone rang. As she answered, she walked away from the noise of the bar as best she could.

'Hello, Huda,' she said.

'Ravi, where are you?' her friend demanded.

'I'm downstairs.'

'In the theatre?'

'Yes. Where are you?'

'I'm right outside!'

'Okay, I'll come up.'

She pocketed her phone and headed for the stairs. Outside, she found a smart black limo waiting for her. Two drones followed her from the front of the theatre to the car door. They moved to above and behind the rear window as she climbed inside.

Huda Jellicoe was sitting in the car alone holding a flute of champagne, a slight woman about twenty-five years Ravi's junior. Ravi couldn't see the driver. Huda handed her a glass of her own. She was laughing.

'I can never get over how you have drones following you everywhere!' she exclaimed.

Ravi gave her a resigned look.

'Perks of the charity sector,' she said.

'You're like a gangster. It makes you mysterious.'

'Hardly.'

'Where were you, anyway?' Huda asked her. 'I saw the others leaving ages ago.'

'They were heading straight for the house. I needed a break from them so I went for a drink first.'

'On your own?'

'Yes.'

'Ravi, you are funny.'

Ravi examined her champagne and looked around the limo.

'Bit over the top isn't it?'

'We're at the *opening night…* with the *President* attending.'

'You didn't even come in to see it!'

Huda pulled a face.

'It's a depressing play.'

Ravi took a sip. Huda gestured for the driver to start moving. Their destination was not far and it was a warm, late August evening – they could have walked if they had wanted to, but Huda would never have wanted to.

'So what was it like?' Huda asked.

'Actually it was very good.'

'Could you see the President?'

'She was in her box. Everyone could see her.'

'Who was she with?'

'Just Pilcher. Pilcher and six androids.'

'Six!'

'With their eyes fixed on the audience the whole time.'

'Well, I shouldn't think they were interested in the play. I wonder if she'll come to the house.'

'Giselle seemed pretty confident she would.'

'Yes, but you know what it's like. Busy important people.'

A short time later the limo pulled up in front of a tall townhouse in the heart of Chelsea.

'Here we are,' Huda said.

Ravi showed her friend her mostly untouched champagne.

'What do I do with this?'

Huda inserted it into a neatly secure slot on a little shelf to the side. Her own empty glass was already beside it.

'I'm a bit nervous!' Huda said.

'You know almost everyone here!'

'But the President!'

'You'll mostly be watching her from across the room, Huda.'

'I suppose so.' Huda looked disappointed.

They climbed from the limo and walked a thin pathway to a front door at the top of a short flight of steps. Ravi's drones hovered in the front garden.

'Will they stay there all night?' Huda asked.

'If they're good.'

'They're not very discrete. What will the President think?'

'She knows all about them.'

'She does?'

'Of course.'

They rang the doorbell. A young woman – a human maid – opened the door.

'Huda Jellicoe and Ravinder Babbington,' Huda said.

An android standing behind the maid scanned their faces and confirmed their identities.

'This way,' said the maid. She led them straight ahead, down a long, wide hallway lined with paintings by mostly living artists to a huge, circular room that at the moment was the party room. It was impossible to tell what its function was on a normal day – perhaps it was always a party room. It was filled with about fifty people, the great and the good – Ravi was acquainted with about a third of them, Huda knew at least half of them. In the doorway, a serving droid presented them with a tray of glasses. As Ravi took one and inspected it, trying to identify the liquid inside, Giselle Barsby – owner of the Royal Court Theatre and host of the party they now attended – swept towards them.

'Huda! Ravinder! I'm so glad you made it!'

'Wouldn't miss it,' Huda said. 'Is she here?'

'Not yet, sweetheart. Be patient. What did you think of the play?'

'Um,' said Huda.

'I loved it,' Ravi told her.

Giselle beamed.

'I'm so glad. Do you know it's the first production of *Death of a Salesman* for fifty years? I should introduce you to the direct – ' She looked over her shoulder. 'Oh, she's busy. Well, you don't need me to hold your hand, I'm sure you know everyone here. Come on in!'

And she was gone.

Ravi and Huda looked at each other.

'Satoshi Pilcher's not here either,' Huda said despondently.

'This new fascination with politicians!' said Ravi.

'It's not the politics, it's the…' She trailed off.

'Who shall we talk to?' Ravi asked her.

They surveyed the room.

'Adebayo's over there,' Ravi pointed.

Huda turned down the corners of her mouth.

'Trust you to want to talk to a civil servant.'

'He's my friend.'

'Okay.'

They crossed the room. Adebayo, a gentle-looking character in his early seventies, wearing what looked like the same suit he wore to work, was alone, looking at a collection of books tucked into a small alcove.

'Mingling well, I see,' Ravi said.

Adebayo turned, surprised, smiling when he saw who it was.

'Hello, Ravi, Huda,' he said.

'Not the party type?' Huda said.

Adebayo sighed.

'I'm just here to show my face,' he said. 'The President asked if I would be here.'

'But she's not here,' Huda complained.

'She will be. She'll arrive late, after the Chancellor.'

'He's not here either.'

Adebayo laughed.

'Within the hour,' he said, 'they'll both be here.'

'I didn't see you at the play,' said Ravi.

'I didn't see you,' he countered.

'I was in one of the boxes.'

'I was in the cheap seats.'

'The cheap seats!' said Huda.

'Adebayo prefers to sit with the real people,' Ravi said. Adebayo laughed again.

'What did you think of it?' he asked her.

'I think it's a weird play to show in this day and age. It's a weird play for the President to go and see.'

'They like to think about how bad things were before the revolution.'

'Yes, but that's usually – '

'Huda!' said a deep, male voice.

All three turned. A short, stocky man with thinning hair had appeared beside them.

'Burt!' Huda cried, hugging him. 'This is Burt Mears, one of my brother's business partners. Burt, this is my dear friend Ravi Babbington – she owns the O'Keefe Gallery.'

'Pleased to meet you,' Burt said as they shook hands.

'And this is Adebayo Oxley, Head of the Department of Social Welfare.'

'Adebayo and I know each other,' Burt said warmly. The two men shook hands.

'You were talking about the play?' Burt said.

'That's right,' said Huda.

Burt whistled.

'Business was a harsh affair back then,' he said.

'There was no cushion of citizenship,' Ravi agreed.

Burt looked at her briefly, questioningly.

'That's right. It was dangerous and unpredictable.

Makes you wonder who in their right mind would even bother in those conditions. No safety net at all!'

'Have you met the director?' Adebayo asked him.

'Oh yes, she's here isn't she.' Burt looked round. 'Where is she?'

'Over there,' Huda pointed. 'The woman with blue hair and crystal earrings. Monique Collard.'

'Oh yes – yes, I've met her before. Nice lady.' Burt turned back to the group. 'But a bit radical,' he smiled.

'Really?' said Ravi.

'Well… isn't she the one who did *A Midsummer's Night Dream* and the mechanicals were all payers, and Queen Titania fell in love with a payer with a donkey's head?'

'Oh yes, I remember that.' Huda laughed. 'It caused quite a row.'

'And here she is, putting on a play for the President,' Ravi said drily, surprised at what passed for radical.

'Talking of politics,' said Burt, 'all set for the local elections, Adebayo?'

'That's almost a year away,' Huda interjected.

'Still…' said Burt.

'The PON are quite relaxed about them,' Adebayo said. 'I bet they are!'

'Everything's on schedule as far as I'm aware,' Adebayo continued. 'I'm not particularly involved.'

'I thought the PON didn't stand in local elections,' said Huda, confused.

'They don't,' Adebayo confirmed.

'The Liberals are doing very well,' Burt said.

'They are. But they're not a concern.' Adebayo looked closely at Burt. 'Are they worrying you?'

'Not remotely.' Burt emptied his drink and took another from a tray held high by a passing serving droid. 'They're perfectly good for business. Which reminds me – charity regulation, that's you, isn't it?'

'That's right.'

'Are you going to start talking business?' Huda complained.

'Not for long,' Burt promised.

'That sounds long enough. I'm going to talk to Tsitsi. Tsitsi!' she called. 'Are you coming, Ravi?'

'I'll stay and talk business for a while,' Ravi said.

'Suit yourself.' Huda left them to pin down her friend.

'Charities,' Burt said when she was gone.

'Go on,' Adebayo invited him.

Another serving droid came by, this time with a tray of canapes. They each took one, mushroom something or other in pastry. Ravi wasn't keen.

'I'm setting up a charity providing sports facilities for payers,' Burt said. 'There's nothing in the law about payers and amateur sports, but they don't have the spaces and they can't afford the equipment. We want to set up special payer sports facilities. There's a place in Cornwall we're starting off with.'

'Interesting,' said Adebayo. 'Ravi's the one you should talk to.'

Burt raised his eyebrows, turning to Ravi.

'Really? Why's that?'

'Ravi works with payer charities in Turpin.'

'Do you?'

'And Gate,' Ravi added.

'What kinds of charities?'

'Food banks, mostly, and education for payer children.'

Burt was surprised.

'Education? What for?'

Ravi took a deep breath.

'For its own sake. But also,' she went on, 'because at any moment they could be designated a citizen, and if that happens they'll need resources.'

'Don't new citizens get an education uplift anyway?'

'It's a very steep catch-up,' Ravi said. 'It helps to have a better foundation than state payer education gives. But it's not our primary reason – there's the quality of life and personal resources it gives them.'

Burt reflected for a moment on a world of highly educated payers.

'I'm guessing those drones outside are for you,' he smiled.

'Yes,' Ravi smiled in return. 'They are.'

'But my charity,' Burt said, returning to topic, 'is a little different from that. Although it also relates to quality of life. I saw these payer kids on TV playing football on a building site and my heart went out to them. But Adebayo, giving payers resources without giving them more… the bureaucracy is awful.'

'That's true,' Adebayo said sadly. 'There are some finely tuned grey areas.'

'That doesn't help me very much,' Burt chuckled.

'You just need help with your paperwork,' Adebayo told him.

At that moment a man in his mid-thirties in a sharp, deep blue suit and with very short, neat hair appeared between Adebayo and Ravi.

'Hey, old man,' he said.

Adebayo turned, pleased and taken aback.

'Hello Vrenti!' He gave the younger man a hug. 'When did you get back?'

'Yesterday.'

'Are you staying now?'

'For the rest of the year. We'll see. I might need to pop back in the winter.'

'You're looking well, Paris must suit you.'

'It was alright.'

'Vrenti, you know Ravi, don't you?'

The newcomer and Ravi had met a few times, on occasions like this, and only very briefly. They swapped hellos.

'And this is Burt Mears. Burt, this is Lavrenti – '

'Oh yeah, we've met,' Burt said. They shook hands. 'How are you doing?'

'Not bad at all,' Lavrenti told him.

'Burt's just been whining about bureaucracy,' Adebayo said. 'He wants to set up a payer sports charity and we're making it too complicated for him.'

'Of course you are,' Lavrenti said. 'What kind of sport? Football?'

'Among other things…' Burt began.

'Norwich versus Liverpool tomorrow,' Lavrenti said. 'Clash of Champions. Who do you fancy?'

'Liverpool,' said Adebayo.

'Norwich,' said Ravi.

'I wouldn't like to say,' said Burt.

'Not placing a bet?' Lavrenti asked them.

None of them were. Detecting a lack of enthusiasm for the beautiful game, Lavrenti said:

'A payer charity – that's a sensitive venture at a time like this.'

'Is it?' asked Burt.

'After Parliament Square in April and all the fuss about Justice. It's all the talk in Paris.'

'Not as much here,' Adebayo said quietly.

'It was tricky for a while,' said Burt. 'The government came down pretty hard on Justice. Things have settled down again now. I don't think,' he said, focusing on Lavrenti's point, 'that it will hurt charitable efforts towards payers. It's not their fault.'

'From the data we have, donations towards charities with a focus on payers have gone up,' Adebayo added. 'There's a lot of sympathy for them. People aren't blaming them for Justice.'

'Have you found that?' Burt asked Ravi.

'Yes,' she said. 'We've seen a slight increase – not very dramatic, but a definite increase.'

Lavrenti shrugged.

'It must be the way they tell it in Paris,' he said.

'Not exactly friends of the PON,' said Burt.

'Not exactly,' Lavrenti laughed.

'Are they still talking about restoring the internet?' Burt asked him.

'They're talking.'

'The Chancellor's here,' Adebayo told them.

Burt, Lavrenti and Ravi turned towards the door. Satoshi Pilcher, Chancellor of the Exchequer – the man who was inseparable from President Houghton and her regime, the two of them dominant in the PON for the last fifteen years – stood in the entranceway, flanked by two armed androids.

He was greeted by Giselle and, Ravi saw with a smile, Huda. Pretty quickly the honoured guest was ushered to a snug private corner to be introduced to Monique Collard.

'Shall we go and say hello?' Lavrenti suggested.

Adebayo shook his head.

'If he wants to speak to someone, he'll go to them,' he said. 'Or they'll be summoned over.'

They watched for a minute as the Chancellor smiled and chatted to Collard; then, bored, they turned back to themselves.

'I heard he's going to increase the income cap,' said Lavrenti.

'Where did you hear that?' Adebayo asked him. 'Paris?'

'Are you saying it's not true?'

Adebayo raised his shoulders slowly in a thoughtful, non-committal shrug.

'It hasn't risen for a while,' Burt said. 'It might help with the unrest.'

'It would be an option,' Adebayo conceded.

'I was talking to a guy yesterday,' Lavrenti said. 'He reckoned they should never have ended the Brutalisation.'

'Really?' exclaimed Ravi, shocked.

Lavrenti nodded.

'He reckoned the government has got too soft, there was a "creeping compromise," he said. His exact words.'

'Who was this person?' Adebayo asked.

'Just a guy on the train coming home. He said he was a lawyer. He reckoned that since the end of the Brutalisation, the distinction between a lower wage citizen and a better off payer was too blurred, and that payers were getting too free and too aggressive.'

'There's no such thing as a lower wage citizen,' Ravi snapped.

'Well, you know, relative to other citizens,' Lavrenti said. 'Lower wage, not low wage.'

'Even the lowest paid citizen's income isn't comparable to a payer's income,' she said, flaring up – then remembering how she had to play it here and biting her tongue.

'Well, that's what the guy said,' Lavrenti concluded, in a don't-shoot-the-messenger tone. 'But things *have* got softer over the years, and now Justice have risen up.'

Ravi kept quiet. Justice haven't risen up at all, she wanted to say. But instead she sipped her champagne and waited for someone else to speak.

'They're not rising up anymore,' said Burt, sounding almost regretful. 'I wonder if they'll recover from this.'

'They're not banned,' Lavrenti said.

'No. No, that's true. But without media privileges it's difficult to see how they can operate. How long do you think that will last, Adebayo?'

'The media ban?'

'Yes.'

'I think at least a year,' the civil servant told them. 'Probably two or three. But Justice's biggest problem isn't media access, it's the damage to their reputation. Parties like the Liberals and the Egality Party were happy to be seen to have links with them, but not anymore. Ordinary voters think they're troublemakers.'

Ravi opened her mouth. She wanted to point out that Justice – that the protestors – had been simply standing there. The protest hadn't even begun. She wanted to remind them that the red drones had opened fire unprovoked. But she held back. For a moment she thought Burt was going to say it for her:

'It seems unjust, I have to say,' he said quietly. 'Those Justice demonstrators... they weren't the only ones there. There were other groups, the more extreme ones.'

'You mean Justice have taken the flack for extremists,' Lavrenti nodded sympathetically.

'I don't know – it looks a little that way.'

'The government says Justice itself has been infiltrated,' Lavrenti said.

'Yes, it could be.'

'The President's here,' Adebayo told them, apparently taking on the role of room announcer.

They turned. The President stood in the doorway with one human bodyguard and two armed androids. The human bodyguard was wearing a visor. The President had big hair that touched her shoulders and she wore a loose, green patterned dress that was more homely than presidential. Giselle Barsby shook her hand nervously, almost curtseying. President Houghton smiled warmly – Ravi had always thought that the President had a lovely smile. Then Giselle, the President, the bodyguard and the androids cut a smooth path across the room to where the Chancellor was still talking to Monique Collard. The four androids – President's and Chancellor's – stood in a row behind their masters and surveyed the room, which after an initial hush quietly resumed its chatter.

'You were saying Justice has been infiltrated by other groups,' Ravi said to Lavrenti.

'What? Oh, yes.'

'Which groups are you thinking of?'

'Oh, there are a few, aren't there. The Werkers – that's an old one, I think they're still around. And the Dream League, I read about them in Paris. They're big in London apparently. And there's Alison Clarke, have you heard of her? She lives in exile in France and has a following that calls itself Erase Your Injustice, and they have members here… They're all around, all busy undermining order…'

'You seem to know a lot about them!' Burt laughed. 'I've never heard of any of those!'

Lavrenti grinned.

'I suppose I do. It must be my paranoid nature.'

'You've been reading too many Paris newspapers,' Adebayo told him.

'Maybe,' Lavrenti admitted.

'She's coming over here,' Ravi hissed suddenly.

'What?' said Lavrenti, alarmed.

'The President – she's coming this way!'

The other three looked sharply in the President's direction, then turned away, then looked a second time. President Houghton and a single android were walking towards them.

'Adebayo, hello,' the President said.

'Ms. President,' Adebayo nodded.

'Mr. Mears, I believe we've met.' She held out her hand. Burt shook it.

'Yes, Ms. President – at the Aeronautics Conference last year.'

'That's right.'

She looked briefly at Lavrenti and Ravi and then expectantly at Adebayo.

'Ms. President,' Adebayo said, 'this is Lavrenti Falcon

and Ravinder Babbington. Lavrenti is a long-standing friend of the family and Director of European Exports at PLUTO. Ravi is the owner of the O'Keefe Gallery in Kensington and the Spencer Gallery on the South Bank.'

The three of them went through a sequence of greetings and shaking hands.

'The Spencer Gallery,' the President said. 'I saw the Emin retrospective there last year. Fascinating. A harrowing illustration of the discarded past.'

'Yes,' said Ravi, thinking that that wasn't the point of it at all. 'It was a very successful show – we were very proud of it.'

President Houghton looked around the group.

'And what were you discussing before I so rudely interrupted?'

They hesitated. They didn't really want to say – at least, three of them didn't.

'Revolutionary groups that may have infiltrated Justice,' blurted out Burt.

The President was unfazed.

'Really? How interesting. Which groups did you have in mind?'

But now Burt hesitated too.

'Um,' he said.

Adebayo stepped in.

'The Werkers,' he said. 'We wondered how active the Werkers are now.'

Houghton smiled.

'I shouldn't think the Werkers are a serious concern any longer,' she said. 'But what about you, Ms. Babbington?' she said, turning suddenly to Ravi. 'If I remember correctly, your galleries are quite prominent in supporting payer causes in London. Is that right? Education projects, I understand. Presumably that puts you in touch with some of these movements?'

Ravi was taken aback.

'Yes – it can,' she said.

'You needn't be alarmed. My security attachment informed me that a citizen would be here tonight with two drones. Unusual for a gathering like this.' She smiled.

'Yes.'

'So naturally I looked you up.'

Ravi realised then that the President had come to this group not to say hello to Adebayo but to talk to her.

'They're a small inconvenience,' Ravi said, she hoped lightly. 'A necessary, uh, perk of the job.'

The President chuckled politely.

'Yes. So you must know a little about anti-Price groups?'

'A little.'

President Houghton waited. Ravi decided her safest option was to stay as close to the truth as possible.

'The Dream League are very active in London,' she said. 'I've seen, um, signs of their presence – pamphlets and graffiti and so on.'

'Yes, I'm familiar with the Dream League.'

The President waited some more, but this time Ravi kept stubbornly quiet.

'Actually these groups don't concern us very much,' the President said eventually. 'On the whole they are attempts at mass movements that will never get the traction they need. What has happened to Justice is very sad, in many ways they're a perfectly mainstream humanitarian organisation, but they've been infiltrated by Ravi's friends in the Dream League' – she smiled teasingly – 'and others. Now that we've identified that infiltration and nipped it in the bud, I'm sure Justice will be able to return to their more constructive activities soon enough. To tell you the truth,' she said, suddenly lowering her voice and adopting an intimate, conspiratorial tone, even leaning forward a fraction, 'what concerns us more is internal subversion.' Her audience adopted a suitably shocked expression. 'Yes,' she said, looking straight at Ravi. 'Some in government are concerned that disorderly elements have infiltrated... infiltrated, or converted individuals in... parts of the government machine.' She straightened up. 'Very difficult to be sure, of course, and you mustn't get over-concerned about these things. Internal security is very strong. But internal betrayal is a little more difficult to address than a mass movement, which is a relatively straightforward matter to deal with. Have you heard of the Policy of Truth?' she said abruptly, again looking straight at Ravi.

'What?'

'The Policy of Truth.'

'No,' Ravi said.

The President inspected Ravi's eyes for a long moment, then seemed to abandon her search.

'Well – my point really is that it doesn't particularly matter which groups infiltrated Justice, or if Justice became disorderly of its own accord. They're not difficult to deal with, whichever way it happened. But the government must be constantly vigilant about threats closer to home.

Hence, the unfortunate surveillance of well-meaning citizens such as yourself, Ravi.'

Ravi smiled.

'It's a small imposition, really,' she said.

'You're very understanding,' the President said. She surveyed the group. 'I've interrupted you for long enough. Enjoy your evening. See you soon, no doubt, Adebayo.'

Adebayo nodded and the others said goodnight. The President and her android crossed the room to say hello to an actor she'd spotted, Whitney Cole, and beside her, an over the moon Huda Jellicoe.

Ravi's group waited until the President was out of earshot. Ravi let out a long breath.

'What was that all about?' said Burt.

8. LAVRENTI

Eight weeks after the opening night of *Death of a Salesman*, Lavrenti Falcon called in at the reception desk of the Department of Social Welfare. The receptionist was an efficient young man who wore extremely thick glasses – a fashion affectation that Lavrenti found irritating. Nobody needed glasses like that in this day and age. The receptionist made a call, listened through an earpiece and said:

'Mr. Oxley is free to see you right away, Mr. Falcon. He's currently on the seventh floor and has asked you to meet him there.'

'Whereabouts on the seventh floor?'

'It's open plan,' the young receptionist said. 'Mr. Oxley's assistant says he's near the elevators, you can't miss him.'

Lavrenti grunted and walked to the lifts. A short cleaning droid, basically an autonomous vacuum cleaner, was waiting ahead of him. When the lift arrived they slipped inside and Lavrenti waited to see how the two-feet-tall unit would choose its floor. He could have just pressed a button on its behalf but he was curious. The robot waited a few seconds and once it was clear the human wasn't going to help, its top opened and a long, spindly rod extended itself. At the top of the rod was a three-fingered hand; the robot extended its middle finger and pressed the button for the fifth floor. Lavrenti smiled to himself, wondering if it always used its middle finger like that. As the rod retracted, he pressed the button for the seventh.

They stopped at the fifth and the vacuum cleaner trundled out. Alone, Lavrenti fussed with his short hair and adjusted his neat suit in the wall mirror. Stepping out onto the seventh, he saw Adebayo right away, stooped over a circle of desks in a vast, rather noisy open plan office. The room was a sea of circular work stations segmented into four, a person or at least a chair at each segment. In the centre of each circle stood a tower holding screens for each worker, two each, one above the other. Lavrenti didn't like that, he preferred screens side by side. But no doubt there was some reason for it, or some vogue behind it.

Adebayo was leaning over a desk talking with two young women, one seated, one standing. The seated one was showing Adebayo some information on a piece of paper. The one standing was listening carefully and looking occasionally at the uppermost of the desk's two screens. Lavrenti noticed that the seated woman's trousers had hitched up above her short boots and that the skin revealed there was bright, almost reflective metal: robotic legs.

Lavrenti walked towards them and stood at a polite, unintrusive distance.

'Adebayo,' he said quietly.

The old man looked up quickly as though surprised – then relaxed.

'Hello, Vrenti,' he chuckled, standing straight. 'Just ironing out some troubles.'

Lavrenti smiled and nodded at the young women, who were clearly wondering who he was.

'Everything alright?' he said.

'Oh, fine,' Adebayo said. 'Technical issues. Access permissions to some files aren't working as they should. Something needed my signature.' He sighed. 'I used to understand these things much better than I do now.'

'Technology,' Lavrenti said.

'Never stays still.' Adebayo turned back to his colleague seated at the desk. 'Thank you, Yiyun,' he said. 'Is that everything you need from me?'

'I think so. That should do it,' she said.

'Okay then.' He turned to the other. 'I have a meeting now with Mr. Falcon, Betsy, and then I'm off to the committee, but if you need anything, let me know.'

Betsy nodded firmly.

A couple of minutes later Adebayo and Lavrenti were back at the lifts. Another vacuum cleaner was waiting. Was it the same one? Lavrenti wished he'd taken the trouble to notice its markings. Inside the lift, he wanted to see what the robot would do but Adebayo casually tapped the button for the tenth floor before it had a chance to do anything. They began to climb.

'I saw your parents at the weekend,' Adebayo said.

'Mum told me,' Lavrenti replied.

'They seem well. Your Dad's talking about retiring.'

'He's always talking about retiring,' Lavrenti scoffed. 'He'll never do it. He wouldn't know what to do with himself.'

'I don't know. He seemed quite sure.'

'That's because he has that suitcase business with Kitty,' Lavrenti said. 'When he talks about retiring, what he really means is quitting the presidency of Levy and just doing his little side rackets full-time.'

Adebayo chuckled.

'He did talk a lot about suitcases.'

'I bet he did.'

They reached the tenth floor. The robot trundled ahead and the two men walked in easy silence to Adebayo's large office. At one end sat Adebayo's desk, sideways to a long, tall window that let in plenty of blue and cloudless sky. Arranged spaciously in front of the desk were two sofas facing each other over a wide coffee table, and facing the window were a couple of stiff-backed armchairs. As Lavrenti closed the door behind them, Adebayo walked past a battered and out of place looking metal filing cabinet to an equally incongruous – because very old-fashioned – mahogany cabinet. He opened the cabinet wide and said, 'What would you like?'

'Whisky.'

Adebayo poured and Lavrenti walked to the window.

'This office is new,' Lavrenti said.

Adebayo frowned.

'Is it?' He tried to remember. 'Yes, since you were last in this building I've moved down the hall. But that was a year ago, is it that long?'

'Must be.'

Adebayo joined his younger friend at the window with two glasses. They clinked and sipped and admired the view. Eventually Lavrenti said,

'So I'm here because I need an appointment with Mercer.'

Adebayo looked mildly pained but unsurprised.

'I thought so,' he said.

'Can you arrange it?'

'Is this about the PLUTO office in Sweden?'

'Yes. It's getting annoying.'

Adebayo was thoughtful but said nothing.

'Can you set it up?' Lavrenti asked.

Adebayo nodded.

'I think so. How quickly do you need to see her?'

'As soon as possible. The contracts need to be signed by the end of October.'

'She's in Kenya. I can call her but I can't get you a meeting until next week.'

'I don't need to see her in person. Satellite link is fine.'

'You know how the government feels about satellite links. I can't get that for something like this.'

Lavrenti harrumphed quietly.

'Will next week be too late?' Adebayo asked him.

'No, that can work.'

'Will anyone else in the Foreign Office do? Miller? Jenny?'

Lavrenti shook his head.

'It needs to be Mercer. I've spoken to Miller already, he's sympathetic but he doesn't have the authority. Only Mercer can get the Swedes to give us the permits.'

'Yes – I thought as much.' Adebayo sighed. 'Well,

Vrenti, I'll call her today. What time is it? It's about 5.30 in Kenya. I'll call her in the evening.'

Lavrenti seemed to relax a little.

'Thanks, Addy.'

'I can't promise she'll give you what you want.'

'That's fine. I just need a chance to talk to her.'

'I'll let you know tonight what she says. If she's agreeable, most likely Jorge will call you. That makes it unofficial.'

'Alright,' Lavrenti nodded.

They turned again to the view, brief business concluded. Lavrenti regarded the armchairs but decided to stretch his legs round the office instead.

'This is bigger than your last room,' he said.

'Yes, a little bit. Warmer too. The heating never worked in the other one, I don't know why.'

Lavrenti hovered by Adebayo's desk and looked idly over the paperwork scattered around a dusty keyboard and a rather small monitor. Among the print-outs and reports something caught his eye and he picked it up.

'What's this?' he said.

'What is it?' Adebayo asked him mildly.

Lavrenti held aloft a small, slightly creased grey pamphlet.

'It says, "The Truth About The Price".'

'Aah, yes.' Adebayo paused. 'That's interesting. It's a revolutionary pamphlet.'

'Really?'

'An anti-Price polemic,' Adebayo confirmed.

'Why have you got it?'

'People in my position need to be familiar with material of this kind.'

'Is it a Justice thing?'

Adebayo smiled.

'Would you call Justice revolutionaries? No, we believe it's a Dream League document.'

'The Dream League?'

'Yes.'

'These are illegal.' Lavrenti seemed scandalised.

Adebayo raised his shoulders slowly and lowered them again as he spoke.

'Well... it's a grey area. But I have a licence to look at these things.'

'A licence?'

'Not a literal licence,' Adebayo chuckled.

Lavrenti put down his drink and flicked through the pamphlet's pages.

'Have you read it?'

'I have. It's well written.'

Lavrenti read a few lines.

'I suppose you have to keep an eye on these people. How widespread is this stuff?'

'In London, it's everywhere.'

Lavrenti continued reading.

'You must have seen pamphlets like that around,' Adebayo said. 'They turn up on the shelves in supermarkets, on tables in pubs, on seats on the tube...'

Lavrenti shook his head.

'I can't say I have. I rarely get the tube.'

'Well, if you did, you'd come across these.'

'Is that where you found this one?'

'No, I was given that copy.'

'How effective are they, do you think?'

Adebayo shrugged.

'It's small fry. I imagine most people respond to it as you have just done. A few may read it. Even fewer may find it persuasive. Though the evidence is that such sentiments are growing, as far as we can tell.'

'The government are more worried about subversives on the inside than things like this,' Lavrenti observed, repeating what he'd heard from the President a couple of months ago.

'So they say,' Adebayo said. He looked around the room and then lowered himself into an armchair with a stiff-kneed sigh. 'I'm not sure the two can be separated so easily.'

As Adebayo sat down, Lavrenti perched on the edge of the old man's desk.

'I don't know what they think they would do differently,' he said.

'You mean the people who wrote that pamphlet?'

'All of them,' Lavrenti said dismissively.

'Well,' Adebayo said slowly. 'Justice, for one, would simply remove the Price. Everyone would climb or fall as their fortunes and their talents decided. The people at the bottom would be selected, as they would put it, naturally.'

'I know what Justice think,' Lavrenti said. 'They want to go back to before the wars. When it was chaos.'

'It wasn't chaos, exactly. But it was unstable, that's true.'

'But what about the others? The Dream League?' Lavrenti raised the pamphlet briefly, still held in his hand. 'What does it say in here?'

'Revolutionaries of the Dream League's ilk believe that nobody needs to pay the Price at all. Everybody can be a citizen.'

Lavrenti scoffed.

'The rich have too much,' Adebayo added, 'and that's why the poor have too little.'

'It's childish,' Lavrenti said. 'What do they say in detail? Do they say how no one would have to pay?'

'They have ideas… old ideas, mostly. Redistribution. Common ownership.'

Lavrenti knocked back some of his whisky and stared into his glass. He seemed irritated.

'You know,' said Adebayo after a few moments, 'there's a theory put forward by a philosopher called Lawrence Culver that payers really do deserve to pay the Price, because if they had sufficient strength of character, work ethic or talent, they would find a way out. Culver believes there's a whole class of citizens who are actually payers, who succeeded in finding their way into citizenship through a black market in fake identity documents. And he also believes there are many payers who are actually wealthier than many citizens, through organised crime, secret bank accounts, and so on. He even thinks that many members of payer communities like the River of Life have surreptitiously become rich right under the nose of the government's finance surveillance. He claims that the only payers who are truly paying the Price are the genuinely undeserving – that many who are nominally payers are in fact not paying at all.'

'So he doesn't think…' Lavrenti began, making connections.

'He doesn't think the Price is really arbitrary at all,' Adebayo concluded for him. 'He accepts that the *system* is arbitrary, but that the only individuals paying the Price are those without the ability or not making the effort to avoid it. Resourceful people find a way. Although he does admit that many citizens lack those qualities too and are protected from the consequences.'

Lavrenti thought this over.

'That contradicts the basic principle,' he said.

'Yes. It philosophises merit back into the system. And it claims that what Justice wants has already been achieved.'

'What do you think of that?' Lavrenti asked.

'I think… many think that Culver can't stomach the arbitrariness of the Price and has devised a rationalisation that lets him live with it.'

'Sounds about right. Is there any evidence of these black market citizens or these rich payers?'

Adebayo laughed.

'No. By definition they're all hidden, very conveniently. But in a society as closely watched as ours, I think it's very unlikely. Perhaps a tiny handful…'

'Not many,' Lavrenti agreed.

He put the pamphlet, which he had been holding all this time, back on the desk.

'What these people forget is the history. They forget the chaos that led to the wars and why we need control.'

Adebayo gestured with his glass towards the abandoned pamphlet.

'I'd like to know what you think of another argument it makes,' he said. 'I think you'll feel strongly about this, Vrenti. The author says that the Price applies arbitrarily to each individual – we are designated citizens or payers. But newborn children are not subjected to a designation process. We inherit our parents' designation. So, in fact, we have the appearance of an arbitrary system but what we actually have is an underclass of born payers.'

Lavrenti took a deep breath but said nothing.

'It's relatively rare for citizens to be designated payers these days,' Adebayo continued. 'The balance in the population is stable and there's no need for large numbers of redesignations. But designations the other way round,' he said gently, 'are even fewer.'

Lavrenti circled his glass in both hands.

'But it does happen. I'm living proof.'

'Yes. But it's rare, Vrenti.'

'It's rare,' Lavrenti conceded. 'But when it happens… my parents and my sister were made citizens along with me, because I was still an adolescent. Four of us. That doesn't happen when you pay, the government doesn't drag your family down with you. But it does help you lift them up.'

Adebayo nodded kindly.

'But the fact remains, Vrenti, that about a fifth of the population is born into paying.'

Lavrenti shrugged indifferently.

'There may be some truth to it. But the point is, the root cause is arbitrary designation. And things don't stay still. I was made a citizen at sixteen, other citizens are made into payers. In any case, it comes back to the fundamentals – it's no different to the old ways, but the Price is honest, and stable. There are no good reasons for anyone to be at the bottom, except that someone has to be at the bottom.'

Adebayo smiled and finished his whisky.

'And there is the difference with our author,' he said. 'They would say there are no good reasons for anyone to be at the bottom, because nobody has to be at the bottom.'

Lavrenti laughed briefly.

'There you have it,' he said.

He drained his own glass.

'Do you spend a lot of your time debating in your head with these people?' he asked.

It was Adebayo's turn to laugh.

'More than I should,' he said.

Lavrenti shook his head.

'I wouldn't have the patience.'

'You're a practical businessman,' Adebayo told him.

'That's right.'

Lavrenti lifted himself from the desk and stretched.

'Time to go,' he said.

'Yes,' said Adebayo, standing. 'And I'd better do some work.'

He escorted his young friend to the door. In the doorway they hugged and Lavrenti said:

'So you'll let me know how it goes with Mercer as soon as you can?'

'I'll call you tomorrow,' Adebayo promised. 'Though you may hear from Jorge first, he's very efficient.'

'Thanks, Addy. I'll see you soon.'

'See you soon, Vrenti. Take care.'

Adebayo watched Lavrenti as he walked down the corridor and called the elevator, a cleaning droid running behind as though following him. Then the old man closed the door to his office and walked back to his desk. He picked up the pamphlet and slipped it beneath a pile of papers so that no other visitor would see it.

9. ADEBAYO

Nine weeks after putting Lavrenti in touch with the Minister for Foreign Affairs, Adebayo Oxley called his driver. It was 7.30 in the morning and Adebayo was already in his office, clearing a few messages and picking up some paperwork he'd forgotten the night before. Adebayo had always been an early riser. He slept less than he used to but even as a young man he had always been an early to bed, early to rise kind of person. Not much of one for partying.

He told his driver he'd be down in two minutes and left his office. He locked it carefully behind him, a habit he had picked up only recently. He knew that others had too. It might look suspicious, but everyone was so paranoid these days it would actually look odd if he *didn't* lock it. He used not only the keypad but also an actual metal key. He understood, though, that of all the people likely to be under suspicion, he was very far down the list. He was too old, too venerable, and simply not taken seriously enough. Loyal, rusty Adebayo, overdue for retirement.

He took the lift to the ground floor and left by the main entrance. Even Sal, the receptionist with the big glasses, wasn't in yet; the only bodies Adebayo saw on his way out were security droids either side of the front door. He nodded at them as he passed. Outside, his driver sat waiting in the car and he let himself into the back, dropping his briefcase and a cardboard folder onto the seat beside him.

'Okay, Mina,' he said. 'Let's go.'

Without a word Mina began driving. She had brought him here from home and had been up at least an hour before he had. But Mina was not a morning person. As they glided away from Whitehall, Adebayo took pity on her and said:

'Have you had breakfast yet, Mina?'

She gestured lightly towards the passenger seat beside her.

'I have something here with me, sir.'

'If you want to stop along the way…'

'Thank you, but I doubt I'll need to.'

'Alright.'

They made this journey once a month but not usually this early. Adebayo had not given Mina a reason for the new timetable and she had not asked for one.

They settled into the trip. Adebayo opened his briefcase. He had a few things he was supposed to read, but nothing very exciting. He pulled a slim wad of documents onto his lap, but after just a few minutes found his mind wandering, worrying. He gave in to it – put the paperwork aside and allowed his thoughts to occupy him as he gazed through the window at passing London.

They were going to Cheltenham, to the Citizenship Data Centre – a routine part of his job, but not a strictly necessary one. He could just as easily delegate it or, in his position, have someone from the CDC come to him in London. In fact, he used to do both those things and only made the trip to Cheltenham himself once or twice a year. But for the past couple of years he had taken to going in person, to talk to Bano or somebody else face to face and to spend some time looking at the data directly. His staff generally put it down to an ageing senior official's whim, even eccentricity, and a desire to indulge himself in some hands-on technicalities as a respite from the burden of management. And he did enjoy these visits, did enjoy immersing himself for a few hours in practicality and detail.

But on his mind today, as they left Westminster, were the troubles of the times. In the months since the Parliament Square attack, and even more so in the past few weeks, the government had grown more unstable than at any point in Adebayo's adult lifetime. Paranoia was consuming the centre, seeping into every relationship, every interaction, every decision – most of it emanating from the President herself, and all of it stemming from the Policy of Truth: a name and a notion about which the President knew almost nothing, an almost nothing that was tearing the government apart. Adebayo sometimes thought that the Policy of Truth hardly needed to exist – just the rumour of its existence was harm enough.

The PON was used to resistance. It had seen opposition

parties and leaders come and go. It had seen revolutionary and democratic movements spark into life, flower and flourish, then crumble or fade away. Over the years the PON had loosened, not tightened its grip, as it grew more confident in its power and in the futility of moves against it. It had allowed the River of Life to develop its networks and communities, it had allowed political groups to emerge from it, it had even turned a blind eye to low-level, illegal payer unionisation. All of these things softened the burden on payers and only served to stabilise the order that was the PON's fundamental goal. The population's desire for the security that the PON gave them, the government's control of media, the crazy levels of surveillance on continual display, the PON's knowledge (they believed) of so much of resistance activity neutralised any serious threat.

But then President Houghton learned of the Policy of Truth: a movement, anti-Price, within the government itself. There was scant evidence – a note discovered in a rubbish bin, a conversation recorded by an android in a bar, the confession of a junior civil servant who revealed very little and then disappeared. But it was enough – the President became convinced very quickly that a shadowy group of senior politicians and officials were working against her, against the Price, against the PON. What were they doing? What were their goals? Who were they? Who were they connected to? Nobody knew. Nobody could find anything. There was no evidence of either subversion or sabotage. Errors, incompetencies, communication failures, which were abundant, began to be taken as signs of Policy of Truth activity. Was co-ordination between different ministry's drones so poor because of complexity, resourcing and inefficiency, or was the hand of the Policy at work? Was the shutdown of all surveillance cameras for fifteen minutes at Waterloo Station in the spring of last year, for example, a power outage or Policy vandalism?

There was no way to know. The innermost circle of government was convinced the Policy of Truth was all around them. The President was reluctant to assign visible surveillance to her own ministries for fear of how it would look and for fear of provoking the Policy before she had more understanding of who and what they were. How many levels of government did the Policy already control? Adebayo had no doubt that government officials and ministers at every level, including himself, were under *secret* surveillance, but there were no drones, no cameras, no androids. Instead, the President lashed out at a target she *did* know – Justice. Hence the attack on Parliament Square, the clampdown on Justice's leaders and freedom, the glut of spy drones in Turpin. It was designed to send a message: we know you're up to something, and if you threaten us, we will be ruthless.

It didn't much help. Did the Policy of Truth even have any connection to Justice? Justice members interrogated about it seemed bewildered. Was there any indication that the Policy was at all chastened or weakened by Justice's downfall?

Adebayo feared that some violent move was not far away. Arrests, accusations, attacks were only around the corner. Ravi Babbington, Adebayo knew, now had ten drones and the accounts of her galleries and charities subjected to monthly audits. The Dream League had been banned, a few senior members arrested and every associated individual assigned half a dozen drones each as well as, in some cases, actual androids. Drones never went into buildings but androids did – into your workplace, into every shop you entered, every pub you visited. There were reports of androids entering people's homes and standing sentry outside their rooms; of androids following suspects into bathrooms. Turpin and Gate, the largest payer regions in London, felt a lot like prisons now, with armed robot guards five to a street. Adebayo had also heard – in fact he had seen the documents – that many of the new drones hovering over heads in Turpin and Gate were red drones. What did the PON intend to do with those?

A nascent illegal union in Gate had been shut down. A proposed rise in the income cap had been cancelled – the funds were needed, the Chancellor said, to fund the extra security demanded by the rise in rebellion activity. News reporting about Justice had taken a distinctly more hostile tone. There was even talk – in whispers – of a second Brutalisation.

Adebayo churned these things over in his mind, worrying, speculating, until he realised he was going round in circles and needed to stop. Still unable to focus on work, he decided to sleep, slipping a pillow behind his head and settling back for the last hour or so of the trip. He asked Mina to put some music on and fell into a doze surprisingly easily.

When they arrived at the CDC, Mina had to nudge him awake. 'We're here, sir,' she said twice, more loudly the second time. Adebayo stirred to find himself leaning awkwardly between the back of his seat and the window, with a stiff neck. He straightened slowly. Outside lay vast stretches of car park. Beside him stood the entrance to the large, bright white, circular building that housed the CDC.

Adebayo rubbed his face and picked up his briefcase.

'Thank you, Mina,' he said. 'I'll call you in a few hours.'

'See you later, sir,' she said.

Walking to the entrance, he thought he detected some movement over his shoulder and turned quickly, expecting to see a drone. But there was nothing. He passed through a heavy glass door into a quiet, marble-floored lobby – a rather echoey space filled with lounge chairs and low tables. Professionals in suits milled about like figures in a brochure by the building's designers. He headed straight for the reception desk and said:

'Adebayo Oxley for Bano Huston.'

It was 10.00. He was half an hour early, but Bano wouldn't mind about that. The receptionist was a robot – not the functional, metallic kind Adebayo was used to, but one of the plastic types with smooth bodies and animation faces that he found creepy. Models like this were relatively rare, because expensive, but you often found them in places like reception areas and hotels because they were believed to be more approachable. Adebayo preferred a machine to be a machine.

'She will be with you in two minutes,' the receptionist said, presumably after having made contact through internal comms, since it hadn't moved or touched a thing.

'Thank you,' Adebayo told it and stepped a few paces away while he waited. Sure enough, two minutes later a young woman was striding across the lobby towards him – Bano Huston, CDC Director of Data Analysis. He liked and admired Bano, but even after all his years Adebayo was nonplussed when people as young as she was reached such senior positions. He wasn't really sure how it happened. He sometimes reflected on how the Price had built a wall around the poor and contained them, but hadn't changed much else. The vagaries surrounding who reached the top were in some ways much the same as they ever were. He remembered a Dream League pamphlet sarcastically proposing an inverse of the Price to install people at the top. It had named it 'the Award.' The next time he saw Lavrenti he would suggest it and see how he reacted.

'Hello, Adebayo,' Bano said, kissing both his cheeks. 'How was your drive?'

'I slept most of the way,' he confessed. 'I'm getting old.'

'You're early.'

'Yes. It's a busy time.'

'Shall we go up?'

They took an elevator to her office. There, they sat side by side at a small round table and looked together at figures on Bano's laptop. These meetings were always brief – they rarely lasted more than an hour. Afterwards, Bano would take him round the complex to say hello to half a dozen members of staff; then the two of them would have a coffee; then she would leave him alone to peruse recent data on the EOC 2. This was the ritual Adebayo had developed over the past two years, his oasis from the circus at home and, Bano told him, a nice break from the routine for her too. People at the CDC, she once confided, looked forward to the old man's visits.

On her screen Bano showed him surveillance data, polling data, focus group data, spending data, welfare data, public services data. For forty minutes she gave him a skilfully composed presentation of the social and spending patterns relevant to his department over the past month, the costs, the savings, the improvements, the projections, the risks. They talked briefly about the potential impact of freezing the income cap and about some minor fluctuations coming from the creation and then suppression of the Gate union – but they kept away from the politics of it. Bano said nothing directly about the government's increased surveillance and the restriction of the resistance groups until her closing comments:

'The government's moves have made little difference economically – dissent has decreased, as you'd expect, but there are indications that beneath the surface discontent is growing. Little incidents of individual reaction.'

'Anything to worry about?'

'Not really – not yet. These incidents are dealt with immediately because... because there are androids everywhere now.'

Adebayo thought he might have detected criticism in her tone, but he couldn't be sure.

'I didn't see that in your presentation,' he said. 'What do you have, what do you know?'

'Oh, it's a seam in the surveillance data,' she said, moving back to an earlier screen. 'Reported incidents by androids and drones of verbal or physical aggression directed at them, and reports by firms employing payers concerning outspoken disgruntlement among staff.'

'Outspoken disgruntlement,' Adebayo repeated with a smile.

'That's actually a category,' Bano said, showing him a column of numbers with that phrase as its heading.

'It's a new one on me,' the old man said.

'It came into use four months ago. It's been insignificant until very recently.'

'So there's a slight increase,' he said, leaning a little towards the screen.

'Yes. The category is too new to know what that means. But this isn't organised resistance or formal complaint, this is individuals…' She struggled for a phrase.

'Losing their rag,' Adebayo suggested.

Bano laughed.

'Yes.'

Adebayo leaned back.

'Alright,' he said. 'Something to watch.'

'Yes,' Bano agreed.

That concluded her presentation.

'All fairly stable, considering,' Adebayo said.

'The next few months will be crucial.'

Adebayo hesitated. For a moment he was tempted to talk to her about the atmosphere in Whitehall, about the trouble brewing, even about the Policy of Truth. But he quickly decided against it. He had no idea how much Bano knew, and when it came down to it, for all the warmth between them, he really didn't know her personally all that well. Instead he said:

'Thank you, Bano. Shall we go for a walk?'

Bano smiled. She closed the monitor and gathered up her papers. 'Be warned,' she said. 'When you see Keki, he's going to talk your ear off about his mountain bike.'

'I'd heard about that.'

They left the office and Bano locked it behind her. Did she always do that? Adebayo couldn't remember. They walked together down the corridor, to pay some visits and complete the rest of the old man's ritual.

*

After their coffee, sitting in a staff café overlooking the lobby – which looked much larger from this vantage point, full of people meeting and greeting, going about their business – it was time for Adebayo to turn to the last of his tasks. This one he did alone, so he and Bano said their goodbyes. They parted at the top of an escalator: Bano was going down to welcome another guest, Adebayo was heading towards the inner reaches of the Centre.

'See you next month?' Bano said, glancing over the balcony to see if her appointment had arrived.

'No,' Adebayo said. 'I'm going to be doing the next couple of reviews from London.'

Bano was surprised.

'Why's that?' she asked him.

Adebayo made one of his slow shrugs.

'Things are growing a little… complex in Westminster,' he said. 'I – we – every senior official needs to be on hand. We're a little restricted.'

Bano held his gaze for a moment, concerned.

'Do you want me to come to London?' she asked him.

'No,' he said quickly. 'No, just send your presentation, for the time being. I'll be back after a while.'

'I hope so.'

She smiled and Adebayo smiled in return.

'Well,' said Bano, switching reluctantly to business-like. 'I'd better get on. See you soon, Adebayo.'

They hugged briefly.

'See you soon, Bano,' Adebayo returned.

The Director of Data Analysis let herself be carried down the escalator; the Head of Social Welfare turned and walked to a row of elevators nearby. Alone inside the first tin box that opened, he tapped a personal code into the wall and pressed the lowest in a column of round buttons. The button above it was marked 'B,' but the button he pressed was unmarked.

The lift moved smoothly but slowly. At the basement it hesitated, then continued.

The doors opened into an empty, silent, clinically white corridor. Adebayo stepped out and walked steadily, measuredly, his briefcase at his side, his feet tapping cleanly against the hard floor. The corridor curved rightwards and Adebayo eventually stopped at a door in the inner wall of the curve.

The door was marked 'E.' He tapped his personal code for a second time and went through.

On the other side, the wall, the floor and the ceiling were metal. A faint electronic hum gave the space a sense of concentration and stillness. He was alone here and expected that to remain the case. Opposite him was a row of white lab coats hanging from hooks; he selected one, his own name in its collar, and put it on.

To his left, after a short walkway, the space widened abruptly into a large square. He walked into it and to his right, lining the wall the room expanded along, was a row of neatly tidied desks. At one of them, a small desk lamp had been left shining. Conscientiously, he switched it off.

Along two other walls stood a series of tall, identical machines. They were oblong, about eight-feet high, and made of the same metal as the walls. On the front of each were two large discs, one above the other, that looked like giant film spools. Above the spools were several rows of multi-coloured lights, flashing on and off in an elaborate pattern; below the spools were bewildering arrays of buttons and switches.

Adebayo stood and regarded the machines for a moment. It always impressed him to be here, even after all these years.

This was the Price.

To be exact, this was the machine that separated the population into citizens and payers. It held data on every single individual in the country – here, in these very machines, not on some server elsewhere. It calculated quotas and economic and social patterns, and it designated a percentage of people either citizens or payers according to its calculation of the greatest social stability, economic balance and national prosperity. The number of payers always hovered around twenty per cent of the country – that was loosely pre-set, by the Price's original designers. But within that margin, this machine assigned every person's position – autonomously, automatically and unquestioned.

The machine had several names. Its formal, technical title was the Economic Ordering Calculator (EOC) 2 (it was the second after a crude prototype). But within the CDC, within government, and in the country at large it was also variously called, sometimes fearfully, sometimes cynically: the Calculator, the Computer, the Invoicer, the Lottery. Sometimes it was nicknamed 'Florence's laptop.' Most commonly, across the country, it was simply called 'the Price,' the name used interchangeably both for the system and the machine that implemented it. Much less commonly, but most frequently here in the CDC, it was called 'Elroy.'

Elroy Newbury was the EOC 2's creator, a brilliant technician who, along with the first PON president, Pierce Curzon, had been a leading figure in the electoral revolution that brought the PON to power and one of the architects of the Price itself a decade later. He was generally celebrated as a genius. He had enjoyed total control of the EOC project, from its workings to its outward design. It was because of Newbury that the EOC 2 looked like this – a stylised imitation of chunky, clunky 1950s computers. Elroy loved the early waves of twentieth century computing, the gigantic units that took days to perform a task a modern computer could do in milliseconds, and he paid tribute to them in the appearance of his masterpiece. It was also because of Elroy that everyone who worked in this room wore a white lab coat, even today, years after his death. Many members of the PON fetishized the past in this way, and Elroy was no exception.

Naturally the machine was far more advanced and powerful than it looked. Even now, so many decades after the EOC 2 was first switched on (the ceremonial lever that Newbury and Curzon had pulled, bringing on the lights, stood in the corner behind a rope), no one saw any need to significantly upgrade it. The units Adebayo was looking at now, with their film spools, clicking switches and flashing lights, were a façade. Inside them was one of the most compact and complex computers in the world.

Adebayo approached a unit in the centre of the first row and prepared to engage with the machine's reality. He gripped the lower of the two film spools by its top, pushed aside a latch with his thumb, and eased the spool down by a hinge on its base. Once horizontal, the spool clicked into place to form a circular desk. From a narrow slot at the unit's side Adebayo retrieved and expanded a small fold-up stool. Then, in a reverse of the first spool, he unclipped the upper spool at its base and raised it by a top hinge, until it too was horizontal. He pushed against its edge and the disc slotted neatly into the unit. Now he was sitting at a desk facing a set of four screens. A keyboard had risen from the surface of the desk and, at the back, four small levers each of a different colour: red, blue, green and yellow. He pushed the red one and the lower left screen lit up.

Adebayo set to work. He keyed in his personal code, then a second EOC 2-specific code, then a monthly-updating password. Focused and silent, with the quiet hum of the machines around him, he set about his tasks. The first was fairly basic: he called up the data Bano had used in her brief presentation, to look at the detail for himself, peering at the single screen with eyes that were clear and strong for a man his age. He moved through page after page of figures and columns, backwards and forwards, cross-checking. Others would have used all four screens, but Adebayo found that a little distracting; he preferred to focus on one spot. He saw the same patterns that Bano had pointed out to him – everything significant, she had mentioned. That was as he had expected – Bano was highly skilled and very trustworthy. But it was his job, his responsibility, he felt, to check for himself.

When he was satisfied that he had seen all that he needed to see, he turned to his second task. One of the central principles of the Price was that the line, the distinction, between a citizen and a payer should be clear and obvious. That meant there needed to be a clear space between the lowest paid citizen and the most resourced (you could hardly say 'wealthiest') payer. On the whole, the income laws took care of that and the difference was clear and wide. But grey areas crept in from time to time, between the unluckiest citizens and the more entrepreneurial (or criminal) payers, particularly those buoyed up by the River of Life and others. He did not often discuss it with Bano, but among Adebayo's responsibilities was the erasure of these grey areas, the maintenance of the citizen/payer distinction. He might have to amend the law, he might have to raise the minimum (citizen) wage, he might even have to target individuals or organisations – raise a salary, pay a debt, review a company policy, or, conversely, clamp down on someone's earnings or savings, take them out of their second or third job. Government surveillance, widely mocked for its ubiquity and inefficiency, was especially useful in collecting information in this regard.

He spent a good length of time on this, but found nothing to concern him. He leaned away from the screen, straightening and stretching his back. He stood and walked to an elegant chrome drinks maker in the corner and made himself a hot chocolate.

From across the room he watched the EOC 2 again. Although he had been alive at the time of the Designation (he was five years old), he had no strong memory of it because nobody he knew had been affected. He came from a wealthy family and every friend and relative he had was designated a citizen. But when he thought about it now – when he read about it, watched footage of it, imagined it – he found it chilling. This machine, switched on by Newbury and the president, with various others looking on, in a single stroke, with a few blinks of its cosmetic lights, decided one morning who would be poor. The designation took seconds. The computer produced two numbers: 21.1 per cent and 12.66 million. Over twelve million put into poverty at a stroke. Some were already poor, others not. Some found themselves suddenly lifted into prosperity or something close. But everything that followed, the changes and the enforcements, payers and citizens, the shape of the country ever since – the drones, the control, the Brutalisation, the resistance – all started with this machine, in this room.

He went back to the desk. Putting his hot chocolate in a little indentation at the back designed for that very purpose, he looked in a glazed way at the screen. His mind still on the Designation, he remembered something Ravi had once said about the psychological effects of the Price. Ravi was always talking about the psychology of the Price: she had all kinds of theories. On this occasion, she had been talking about how citizens lived with the knowledge that the Price – the EOC 2 – could strike without notice at any moment. She thought it placed a scar on people. At the time, Adebayo had been unconvinced – it was no different from before, he said, life could go wrong for anyone. As always, all the Price really did was systematise and control what was already the case. Ravi was adamant that the cleanness, the speed, the out-of-the-blueness of the Price was a problem – that the messiness and the process of 'natural' losses softened the blow, allowed time to respond and cope. Adebayo disagreed: the poverty is the issue, he said, not the route to it. You have to contain the poverty, he told her, like any government official would.

He wasn't sure what he thought now.

He placed his hands back on the keyboard. He had one more task. Moving back to the username stage of accessing the system, he typed the same eight digits twice over: 11998929. A new display appeared in front of him, numbers and coding. He pushed the second of the four levers on the desk – the blue one – and the lower right hand monitor came alive. He tapped at the keyboard until that monitor, too, was filled with figures and computer code. He pondered the information in front of him for a few minutes, his clear eyes moving from screen to screen.

He set to work, scrolling through pages, entering queries, typing. He worked more concentratedly than he had before, more purposefully. At times he struggled and frowned, holding data in his head, recalling processes. Occasionally he sipped his hot chocolate or closed his eyes. When he was finished, he returned to the username screen, re-entered his original numbers and password, glanced again through a few screens of information, and logged out of the system altogether.

For a while he gazed at the blank monitors. He turned and looked along the row of units. He rubbed his eyes, knocked back the last of his now cold chocolate, and stood stiffly. He pulled down the upper film spool to conceal the monitors. He raised the lower film spool to close the desk and tuck away the keyboard. He folded the stool and slotted it back into the unit's side.

He threw his empty paper cup into the bin. He picked up his briefcase and looked once more over the room: the EOC 2, the ceremonial lever, the technicians' desks. He walked to the door, shuffling out of his lab coat and returning it to its hook. Then he opened the door and quietly left. He walked the corridor to the elevator, took it to the lobby and left the building, pulling his phone out of his pocket to call Mina as he stood alone in the car park.

10. FLORENCE

Ten weeks after Adebayo's three tasks at the CDC, President Florence Houghton had a call from her secretary on the intercom. It was 9.30 in the morning. It was unusual for Dandan to call her at this time of day, especially with so little in the diary. Florence pressed the respond button and allowed Dandan's face to appear on screen. She looked serious.

'What is it?' Florence asked her.

'Ms. Jay and Mr. Farringdon are here to see you,' Dandan said.

'Really? Why?'

'They won't say, Ms. President. But they say it's urgent.'

Irritated, Florence said:

'Wait a few minutes, then send them in.'

'Yes, Ms. President.'

Florence closed the intercom and turned back to her computer. She wasn't looking at anything sensitive, but she closed her screen all the same. She sat back in her chair to compose herself and wonder briefly what this was about. She wasn't scheduled to see either of them this week as far as she could recall. Naturally her thoughts turned to the negative: security breaches, public unrest, or worse. But if either of those things had happened, she would have heard through other channels, and more immediately than through personal visits. So what was it?

There was only one way to find out. She straightened her back as her door was sheepishly eased open and the tall, elegant Yvonne Jay, Head of Government Security, and the broad-shouldered, no-fuss Leandro Farringdon, Head of the Department of Citizenship, walked into her office.

Florence did nothing to hide the inconvenience of their visit.

'Yvonne, Leandro. What's the matter?'

The two senior officials hovered near the doorway as, to Florence's amazement, a bulky security android plodded in after them. Yvonne closed the door behind it.

'What's that thing doing in here?' Florence demanded.

'Standard procedure, Ms. President,' Yvonne told her. 'The system won't allow us to exclude it.'

They approached her desk and stood before her like teenagers before a headteacher. The android stood behind them. Florence struggled to take her eyes off it. A security unit that was not one of her own bodyguards had never set foot in her office before. She wondered suddenly where her bodyguard was. Of course, it was outside, standing sentry and looming over the unfortunate Dandan as she worked. How had this android been allowed to walk straight past her own guard? Because it was accompanied by the Head of Government Security?

Florence wondered what on earth was going on. She was wrongfooted and she didn't like it. She looked from Yvonne to Leandro to the android. She even read the identity code on the android's chest: DC13A2.

'What's going on?' she snapped.

Leandro cleared his throat.

'Ms. President,' he said slowly. 'We had a communication from the CDC this morning. We don't know how this has happened, but you have been assigned to pay the Price.'

Florence stared at him.

'What?'

'You have been assigned to pay the Price.'

Florence laughed.

'Don't be ridiculous.'

Leandro and Yvonne exchanged glances.

'That's impossible,' Florence said.

'We know,' Leandro told her.

Florence waved at the android.

'So that's why that's here.'

'The system allocates a security unit to every Price designation,' Leandro said. 'It can't be altered, we had no choice but to bring it.'

'Send it outside.'

'We can't do that,' said Yvonne.

'Why not?'

'It has to witness the designation being followed through,' Leandro explained.

'Bring my guard in here.'

'That's not a good—' Yvonne began.

'Bring it in!' Florence shouted.

Yvonne left the office and returned seconds later with a second droid, slightly larger than the first, more polished, more advanced, with a single, stylised P on the left side of its chest.

Florence wondered what would happen if the two robots started fighting.

'Who else knows about this?' she demanded.

'Nobody. I mean – the technicians who saw the original designation, and the three of us.'

'Nobody else?'

'Two technicians called their supervisor, and their supervisor called me. I called Yvonne directly. It hasn't gone any further.'

'Your technicians will keep their mouths shut?'

'They were as shocked as I was.'

That wasn't an answer, Florence thought.

'So what happens now?' she asked them.

'We're looking into it,' Leandro told her. 'The technicians already involved are investigating, but their expertise is limited. To get to the bottom of it, we'll need to tell more people, specialists who can interrogate the EOC 2 system. With your permission.'

Florence slumped in her chair and took a deep breath. She did not give permission.

'And in the meantime?' she asked. She looked from the security droid to her own guard.

'In the meantime, we sit tight and keep quiet until it's corrected,' Yvonne said. 'But we have to follow the process.'

'Follow what process?'

'This unit,' Yvonne said, 'cannot leave until you have paid the Price.'

'What are you talking about?' Florence's voice was rising again.

'We have to inform you that you are paying,' Leandro said. 'We have to provide you with information. You have to demonstrate verbally or through body language that you understand what is happening. Then the unit can leave.'

Florence glared at them.

'It's very brief,' Leandro added.

'It has to be sabotage,' Florence said, ignoring him.

For a moment the other two said nothing. Finally Yvonne said:

'That was our conclusion too.'

'It has to be the Policy of Truth,' Florence said.

'Yes,' Yvonne said quietly. 'That seems likely.'

'How?'

'They must have access to the EOC 2,' Leandro told her. 'Deep access.'

'Someone at the CDC.'

'Or more than one.'

Florence turned to Yvonne.

'Do you have names?'

'We have data on everyone,' Yvonne said. 'My team are looking at it now.'

'They can control the Computer,' Florence said, almost to herself.

'Not control,' Leandro corrected.

The President looked at him sharply.

'No?'

Leandro faltered.

'Not control exactly. Subvert.'

'What's the difference?'

Leandro was silent.

'Call Satoshi,' Florence said abruptly.

'Sorry?' said Yvonne.

'Call Satoshi. Get him here. I don't care what he's doing.'

'What shall I tell him?'

'Don't tell him anything. Just tell him it's urgent.' Florence looked at the two robots in her room, then turned to Leandro. 'You call him. Yvonne, stay here.'

Leandro went outside to use one of Dandan's internal phones. Florence pressed her intercom.

'Dandan, cancel all appointments.'

'Yes, Ms. President,' said Dandan's voice, unquestioningly.

*

Satoshi arrived within the hour. He did not need Dandan to announce him or grant him entry. When he walked into Florence's office, the Chancellor found the President, the Head of Government Security and the Head of Citizenship sitting around a mahogany table at the far end of the room, nursing cups of tea, sunlight from the large window bathing their hands and faces. Two androids stood on one side of the room, blankly facing the opposite wall, their heavy feet no doubt indenting the carpet beneath them forever. The security droid had a blue screen for a face; the presidential bodyguard had a face of simple indentations embedded in hard metal. Satoshi frowned briefly, troubled, at the security droid. As he crossed the room, the President said:

'Satoshi, bring your guard in here.'

He stopped in his tracks, startled.

'Pardon me?'

Florence nodded towards the security droid.

'Just do it,' she said.

Satoshi pressed a pager in his pocket and his own tall robot, a stylised C on its chest and its face another set of indentations, thumped into the room. Satoshi waved and it joined the other two, so that the security droid was flanked by presidential and chancellorship guards.

'Florence, what's going on?' Satoshi said when it was done.

'Sit down, Satoshi,' Florence told him. In the time they had been waiting, Florence had regained her composure and retaken control.

Satoshi obeyed.

'Do you want some tea?' the President asked him.

'Earl Grey,' Satoshi said automatically.

Florence tapped a pad on the desk in front of her but said nothing.

'What's going on?' Satoshi repeated.

Getting a nod from Florence, Leandro filled him in on the morning's excitement. When he had finished, Satoshi said:

'It must be sabotage.'

The others nodded. Satoshi looked over his shoulder.

'Can we discuss this in front of the robot?'

Yvonne nodded some more.

'It's not a particularly sophisticated unit,' she said. 'As

long as it observes the protocol being followed, it won't factor in anything else it hears.'

Satoshi relaxed.

'And only we, and Leandro's three people, know about this?'

'Yes,' Yvonne confirmed.

'Good. Very good.' Satoshi looked at Florence. 'The Policy,' he said.

'It must be,' she said, with steel. 'They've finally moved.'

'They've shown their hand,' Satoshi agreed. 'Surely they've exposed themselves. How many have access to the Computer?'

'Dandan is retrieving the formal list,' Yvonne said. 'But from memory, not much more than fifty people.'

'That many?' Satoshi was surprised.

'The majority of those are CDC technicians, hardware engineers and senior staff. There are levels and avenues of access, they won't all have the same. After that there are maybe a dozen senior government officials. Among ministers only the President, yourself, Ruby Ulrich and Arnold Bradford have unmediated access. Other ministers have access but only when accompanied by an official.'

Satoshi considered for a moment. He turned to Florence.

'What do you think?'

'I find it hard to believe of Arnold,' Florence said. 'Ruby, I'd be surprised but I'm less sure. Of those fifty plus potential suspects, it could be any one of them, frankly. I'm going to increase surveillance on all of them. Even the department heads will be assigned drones.'

'But not the ministers,' Satoshi hoped.

'Of course not the ministers.'

'Assigning drones to department heads will cause a stir,' Yvonne worried.

'I don't care,' the President said. 'There's already a stir. I want them watched. As for Ruby and Arnold, bug their offices and their homes.'

'Are you sure?'

'Everything I say,' Florence announced, 'I am sure about.'

'Very well.'

'The government officials,' Satoshi said. 'Which ones are we talking about?'

'The head of every department concerned with domestic order, economics and security,' Leandro told him. 'And a couple of deputy heads.'

'But few of them have any reason to access the Computer regularly,' Yvonne added.

'Who does access it regularly?' Florence asked them.

'The most frequent users are myself,' Leandro said, 'and Adebayo Oxley.'

'Adebayo,' Satoshi chuckled.

Florence frowned.

'Why is that funny?'

'He's hardly a hacker,' Satoshi said. 'The old man barely knows his way around a keyboard anymore. He's always asking his staff to show him where the files are.'

'He uses the EOC 2 directly every month,' Yvonne pointed out.

'To look at numbers he's already had explained to him,' Satoshi said. 'He doesn't need to go there at all, he just likes visiting Bano Huston.'

'I agree Adebayo is hardly suspect number one,' Florence interrupted. 'He's been in government almost his entire life. But I want him watched too.'

'I'll see to it,' Yvonne said.

'Who else is there?' Florence wanted to know.

Leandro gave a few more names, none of whom struck any of them as particularly likely.

'We'll have Dandan's list soon,' Florence said, closing their speculation. 'The question is, can they be traced?'

'Every use of the EOC 2 is recorded,' Yvonne told her. 'Every user will be identifiable, when they logged in and what they did.'

'So we'll know who's been there,' Florence affirmed.

'The problem is,' Leandro intervened reluctantly, 'we're unlikely to know when the interference took place.'

'What?'

'The instruction to… designate someone a payer… could have been given days, weeks, even months ago. Even years ago. For someone capable of doing this, a delayed instruction wouldn't be difficult. Unless we can find traces of the instruction itself… it could have been anyone who accessed the Computer in the past – well, five years, say, maybe more.'

Florence swore.

'And can you find the instruction?' Satoshi pressed him.

Leandro shrugged helplessly.

'You'll have to ask a technician.'

Satoshi breathed out heavily, exasperatedly.

'But it may be possible,' Florence said. 'It may be possible to trace the instruction, it may be possible to identify irregular use of the EOC 2, it may be possible to identify other signs of subversion or disaffection in our list of suspects. It may be possible to find who did this, or at the very least find a trail back to the Policy.'

'Yes,' Yvonne agreed.

'Get on to it,' Florence commanded, 'the moment this situation is resolved.'

'At some point,' Yvonne said, 'others will need to be told what we're looking for and why.'

Florence shook her head impatiently, as though that was old news and sluggishly obvious.

'Tell who you absolutely need to and only as much as they need to perform their duties. Tell only people you trust. And after you've told them, put them under surveillance.'

'Very well.'

The group fell silent for a minute as the decision settled. At that precise moment, quite neatly, a serving droid glided into the room to deliver Satoshi's tea. As it placed his cup on the desk, Florence wondered how many robots she was going to have to tolerate in her office today. Once the droid was gone, she said:

'As for the sabotage itself – how quickly can this be reversed?'

All eyes turned to Leandro.

'Very quickly,' he said confidently. 'Manual reversal is built into the system. Elroy Newbury in his wisdom didn't leave the EOC 2 impervious to human amendment. We can reverse it today.'

'Who will do it?' Florence asked him.

'The same technicians who reported it. We'll need two codes at senior level, but it will be straightforward.'

'So the codes of any of the four of us will do it.'

'Um – mine, or Yvonne's or Satoshi's… the presidential code will already have been deactivated,' Leandro said apologetically.

Florence pursed her lips angrily.

'We'll drive down as soon as we're finished here,' Satoshi said, sipping his tea. 'Leandro and I.'

'Make sure your technicians never speak of it,' Florence said. 'Give them something – promote them, give them gold pensions, I don't care. But also make them understand the risks.'

'They're loyal citizens,' Leandro said in their defence. 'But yes, I'll do both.'

Florence nodded.

'We have the situation in order,' she said. 'We can reverse this little subversion. We have a small but realistic chance of tracking the sabotage. And we have a defined list of suspects that could lead us to the Policy.'

The group nodded in solemn agreement.

'We may benefit from this,' Satoshi said.

'We may indeed,' Florence agreed.

'The strange thing,' Leandro added, 'is that whoever did this must have known it was reversable. Their intention can't have been to make you into a payer.'

Florence was dismissive.

'Of course not,' she said. 'It's disruption, show of force, threat. The Policy are undermining the integrity of the system all the time. They want to weaken us, chip away at us. Maybe another minister will find themselves getting a call in a week's time. But for now, we reverse this and use what it's given us.'

Leandro cleared his throat.

'Which brings us to the remaining matter...' he began.

'Alright,' Florence sighed. 'Get on with it.'

Leandro raised his voice just a touch, just enough to make sure the security droid could hear. Satoshi and Yvonne kept their eyes awkwardly down, staring into their teacups or at the grain of the desk.

'Ms. President – Ms. Houghton – ' Leandro began. 'You have been assigned' – the security droid seemed to stir slightly – 'to pay the Price. This will take effect in seven days' time, on Wednesday the fourth of March.'

Florence looked at him disapprovingly but said nothing. She glanced briefly at the robots, and again she wondered what would happen if she instructed her guard to resist.

Leandro reached into his jacket pocket and pulled out a small grey booklet.

'Oh come on,' said Yvonne. 'Is that really necessary?'

'It's the procedure,' Leandro said. 'It has to be seen to be observed.'

Embarrassed, he pushed the booklet across the table towards the President. He couldn't reach all the way, so Satoshi leaned forward and slid it across the final stretch. Florence looked at it but did not touch it. The cover said, *Paying the Price: A Guide.*

'This document explains how your new status will be processed,' Leandro said, 'including what will happen to your assets. Most of what is described will be enacted by government. There is very little that you need to do directly.'

He stopped. They waited. Finally Florence said:

'Is that it?'

'That's it,' Leandro said.

Florence thought for a moment.

'And what would a person do next?'

'They'd go home and read the booklet, I suppose. It'll tell them what to do, or what will happen to them. In seven days, their assets are cut to the legal limit and they're on their own.'

Florence nodded. She looked yet again at the security droid. Leandro took it as a hint.

'We can leave now,' he said, standing. 'And take the unit with us.'

'I should stay here with you,' Yvonne said to Florence. 'Until this is reversed, your security access will be affected.'

'Alright. But I'm not leaving this office until this is fixed.' Florence was angry again.

Satoshi pushed back his chair and stepped away from the table. Leandro moved towards the security droid.

'We'll go to Cheltenham,' Satoshi said. 'I'll call you when it's done.'

11. YIYUN

Eleven weeks after the President was assigned to pay the Price, Yiyun Salt called Rosalia's to order some pizza. She made the call from the hallway where it was quieter, then returned to her friends in the front room of her small flat. Ibtisan was sitting on the sofa, Harrison was sprawled almost horizontally across one armchair and Klemens was on the floor, leaning against the sofa's edge with the remote control in his hand, concentrating on the TV. Yiyun flopped down beside Ibtisan and stretched her legs out alongside Klemens. Yiyun's legs were robotic, the result of a car accident in her childhood, and as she crossed one ankle over the other they quietly clinked.

'Half an hour,' Yiyun said, sipping from a cola she'd left resting irresponsibly on the sofa's arm.

'Are we ready then?' Klemens said.

Yiyun had turned twenty five a week ago. She hadn't felt like making a big deal about it and this little get together was a low-key substitute for a party. It was Klemens's idea – it upset him that Yiyun had never seen the early seasons of the greatest television show in history, *Plant Life*, and he had seized the opportunity of her muted twenty fifth birthday to put this travesty right. The whole gang were watching season one together, tonight. Yiyun secretly thought that *Plant Life* – a sitcom about a meteor landing on a garden centre and infecting the plants with an alien bacteria that gave them sentience – was a bit silly, but it was pretty funny and she liked Mr. Oldacre.

'Do it,' Yiyun told him.

Klemens pressed play on episode one: 'Meteor.' As the opening credits rolled, Ibtisan, Klemens and Harrison launched headlong into geeky chatter while Yiyun listened helplessly. They marvelled at how young Jazz was. They explained to Yiyun that Sarita would not appear until season five. They analysed the puppetry of the plants and wondered whether the cacti were the best but also the easiest to do. They discussed continuity, particularly how the plants' apparent confusion seemed inconsistent with claims made in later seasons about a diaspora. They talked over the whole episode, so that by the end Yiyun had barely followed a word. It was supposed to be in honour of her birthday, but in practice she hardly needed to be there – which was how she liked it.

The doorbell rang in time with the first notes of the closing theme tune. 'What did you think?' Klemens asked, but Yiyun was already on her way to answer the door. Her drone, hovering in the corridor outside, inched forward a little when she appeared. She ignored it and smiled at the nervous teenager holding two hot pizza boxes, a cycling helmet sloping loosely to one side of his head. He was wearing a YOURDOORNOW hi-vis vest that was one size too big.

'One Mediterranean and one Marguerita, extra large, for YS?' the teenager said.

'Thanks.' Yiyun handed him two notes. The boy shoved the cash into a pouch strapped to his waist. He started fishing for change, but Yiyun waved that away. Instead the boy handed her a strip of paper and said with an odd emphasis, 'Your receipt.'

'Thank you,' Yiyun replied as she took it.

'Have a nice evening.' He hurried away along the long corridor.

Yiyun stepped backwards into the flat, with the pizzas heating her forearm, and closed the door with her free hand, scrunching the receipt as she did so. She walked to her little kitchen and rested the boxes on the counter. There, in a habit she had cultivated a long time ago, she uncreased the receipt and examined it.

In the top right hand corner, in blue biro, were three letters: OMD.

Yiyun's heart froze.

She looked up, as though someone might be watching, but of course the others were in the living room thinking only of continuity errors. She looked at the receipt again.

OMD.

She didn't know what the letters stood for – she had never been told. But she knew what they meant – she understood the instruction they were giving her. She wanted to go to her room to think, to prepare. Instead, she lifted the pizzas and joined the others.

'Here we go.'

Klemens lifted himself from his cross-legged position to his knees. Ibtisan leaned forward. Even Harrison rose from his half slumber. The four friends dug into their pizzas and Ibtisan went to the kitchen to fetch more colas. Klemens pressed play and they moved on to episode two: 'The Greenhouse.' The others were quieter this time, but still Yiyun could hardly take it in. Her mind was elsewhere.

*

Yiyun woke before the alarm, at 4.47, tired but alert. She washed quickly, dressed, ate a piece of toast, knocked back a glass of water, grabbed a small rucksack and was out the front door by 5.15.

Her drone seemed to take a few seconds to respond to her arrival in the corridor, as though it had been asleep and caught off guard. But it pulled itself together and followed her on the long walk to the stairs at the far end. Yiyun wondered if it would register as suspicious her going into work at this hour. Possibly – but drones tended not to join the dots, they only reported what they saw. The hidden officials who processed the drones' data never seemed to join the dots either.

Reaching the end of the corridor, she walked through some double doors and headed down the five flights of steps to the ground floor. The doors flapped shut behind her. Her patient drone waited until they settled, then extended a single primitive stick to nudge a door open for itself, rotating through the gap and whipping itself downstairs to catch her up. Yiyun liked doing that, she liked being rude to it. On the ground floor, the doors leading out of the building were heavier and involved turning a handle – it took longer for her drone to navigate that. By the time it caught up with her outside, she was already at the station.

This was where they parted company, because even with the ridiculous levels of drone activity these days – even the press were reporting it as a controversy now – drones could still not enter the subway. It just wasn't safe. Yiyun's drone handed her over to transport surveillance and would pick her up again at the other end. She wasn't sure whether the same drone zipped across London to meet her at St. James's Park or whether a different drone already in place took over its duties. She had once inspected her home drone for distinctive markings and found none, not even a scratch. She had also inspected the air for drones torpedoing across town to rendezvous with their targets, but had never seen one going faster than people walked. But she liked to think that it was the same drone that kept her company day and night. It was like a malevolent pet.

The tube was pretty empty and she sat and stared into space from behind her health mask for five stops. She emerged from the station at the other end to find a cloud of drones shuffling above the exit like pigeons around bread. One of them was a red drone. As she walked past them, a single unit separated itself and followed. When her drone had first appeared, weeks ago, she had experimented with dodging and outrunning it. She found she could do that quite easily, but she only tried it a handful of times and always made sure the drone caught up with her. Each time you avoided a drone, someone told her, a red mark went on your record.

The walk to the office wasn't long, less than ten minutes. At her building, she pulled her lanyard from her bag and left her pet waiting among a smattering of others outside. At this hour, the drones loitering outside would be for the security guards and maybe a couple of other early birds. Drones could not enter government buildings. Inside, staff were watched in other ways.

She took the lift to her desk on the seventh floor, joined by a little cleaning droid. 'Where to?' she asked it and a smooth, metallic voice said, 'Fifth floor.' She pressed the button for the fifth and travelled the remaining floors alone.

The seventh floor was empty. Yiyun walked to her desk, not far from the lift: one of a cluster of four, with a two-high monitor tower. She took a seat, dropped her rucksack near her feet, and logged on.

As her computer fired up she looked around, double-checking she had no company. She took a deep breath and focused on the lower of her two screens, centring herself.

The code on the pizza receipt was one of three she could have received. FTG would have been an instruction to stand down until she heard from the Policy directly with new instructions. It would have meant there was some complication, some delay, but nothing fatal. AFE would have been an instruction to cover her tracks and abandon her task altogether – the project had failed, or the Policy had been weakened in some way. But OMD told her that the project had been a success and that she should proceed with her part immediately. It meant that President Houghton had paid the Price, that the government had reversed it and covered it up, and that the government's attempts to trace those responsible had failed. It confirmed that the files Yiyun held, sent to her weeks ago and stored unobserved on her office computer, right under the government's nose, contained records of the entire sequence of events: the EOC 2's designation, the assignment of a security droid, the droid's witnessing of the President's notification, the reversal of the designation by CDC engineers. It was all there.

Yiyun's task this morning was simply to download these files onto a set of memory sticks and send them to a series of destinations. From the outside the most ordinary piece of admin in the world. Still, Yiyun wanted it out of the way quickly, before anyone was around to notice.

By now it was 6.00. Yiyun went to her personal drive and moved from subfolder to subfolder. She opened her desk drawer and pulled a memory stick from a stash piled at the back. The sticks came in more colours than a rainbow. The first she picked was blue.

'Hey, Yiyun. What are you doing here?'

Yiyun whirled round. Walking towards her from the other end of the office was a young woman wearing an alice band and a wide pair of glasses with blue frames. The frames were the exact same shade of blue as Yiyun's memory stick. It was almost as though the memory stick had manifested itself as a person. The young woman carried a clipboard with a thick wad of paper stuck to it.

'Hey, Anwen,' Yiyun said. Anwen worked in Public Communications; they had become friends when Anwen's files got corrupted three years ago and Yiyun was asked to fix them.

'What are you doing in so early?' Anwen asked her, reaching Yiyun's desk and standing over her, looking at the screen curiously. Luckily none of the file names would mean anything to anyone.

'Building up some flexi,' Yiyun said vaguely.

Anwen raised her eyebrows.

'At six in the morning! That's discipline!'

'What about you?' Yiyun asked her.

Anwen held up her clipboard.

'Conference planning meeting,' she said. 'It starts at eight, but as usual there's a million things to do and we have to get the room ready for the ministers. To be honest I don't need to be here this early, but you know what Lavinia's like.'

Yiyun pulled a sympathetic face, but she didn't really know much about Lavinia at all.

'I'm going downstairs for a coffee. Want to come?' Anwen said.

Yiyun looked reluctantly at her computer.

'Um…'

'Go on. You're here now, it still counts as being at work. I'm meeting Tasha.'

'Tasha's here as well?'

'She's doing extra because of the Bluebell Project, they're behind. Colin and Vimal are coming in as well. You chose a good day to come in early!'

Yiyun tried to look as though this was a nice surprise.

'Okay then,' she said. She came out of her folders and logged out of her computer – it would have logged out automatically in three minutes if she hadn't touched it, but she didn't want to leave it exposed even for a second. She grabbed her bag.

*

The canteen was closed but the coffee machine was working and so was the muffin dispenser. Tasha was already waiting, her hair dyed red (it wasn't like that yesterday). They ate blueberry muffins and chatted for half an hour (mostly about hair) before Colin and Vimal turned up, bought muffins of their own and yakked for over forty five minutes. Everyone seemed to find it hilarious that Yiyun had voluntarily come in so early and wanted to know what she wanted the flexi credit for. She talked loosely about a holiday in Italy she wanted to do with Ibtisan and tried to change the subject by telling them about *Plant Life*. They weren't interested in that, but they did thankfully move on to other things, specifically Lavinia, whose management style was apparently a lot more micro than Yiyun had realised. Across the room, a pair of security guards were joking over a cup of tea. On any other day Yiyun would have found it the perfect start to a working morning, goofing off like this with not a manager in sight and the building almost all to themselves. But not today.

Approaching 7.30, all the talk of Lavinia had Anwen starting to worry that she had slacked for too long and ought to get a move on. That set Tasha and the others worrying too. Relieved, Yiyun joined them in the lift and waved them off at different floors: Tasha, Colin and Vimal at the third, Anwen at the fifth. Finally Yiyun was back on the seventh – an hour and a half down the drain, but the remainder still salvageable.

When she got to her desk, Betsy was there, sitting at the next desk along.

It wasn't even Betsy's desk – she usually sat at the manager's cluster further down the room. She looked up from what she was doing.

'Hello, Yiyun,' she said, surprised. 'What brings you in so early?'

Yiyun realised suddenly that she had no idea what time Betsy normally started. When Yiyun got to work at 9.00, her line manager was always already there. She might have guessed 8.30, but she would never have predicted 7.30, even for Betsy.

'Just for some flexi credit,' Yiyun said again. 'Is this the time you always start?'

Betsy sighed with the weight of her responsibilities.

'Sometimes, not always,' she said.

Yiyun sat down. Wary of sounding rude, she said:

'How come you're sitting here today?'

'Oh, there's something wrong with my computer,' Betsy told her. 'IT are coming to look at it later.'

Yiyun nodded, horrified.

'Actually,' Betsy said, 'could you do me a favour while you're here? I can't seem to access my whole profile.'

'Oh, yeah – that happens sometimes,' Yiyun told her. 'It's just the settings.'

She wheeled her chair round to where Betsy was sitting; Betsy shuffled to the side and Yiyun tapped away at her keyboard. But what should have been a two minute fix wasn't working for some reason. She tried this option and that option but couldn't access all of Betsy's folders.

'Should I try a different desk?' Betsy suggested.

'You may as well,' Yiyun said.

They moved to a desk that they knew would be empty

today, on a different cluster. This new desk gave Betsy a clear, unobstructed view of Yiyun's own screen. Betsy logged on and found the same problem, but this time when Yiyun looked at it, she managed to find a solution. She wasn't sure if it was because this computer was working better or because, in her frustration, her brain was getting tense and she had missed things the first time.

At last Yiyun moved back to her desk. It was 8.00.

'Are you coming to the MOC catch up at nine?' Betsy asked her.

'Is that today?'

'Yes.'

'Yes, I'm going to that.'

'Could you give an update on the DD migration?'

'There's nothing to report yet – they're still working on a repository for the yellow files.'

'That's fine, just a general progress report on what's happened since the last meeting and what the main issues are,' said Betsy.

'Okay,' said Yiyun.

That was that. Gathering notes and making them coherent for the MOC people would fill between now and 9.00.

Yiyun set to work.

At 8.30 people started coming into the office, including Geoffrey who sat to Yiyun's left and talked non-stop until Yiyun and Betsy had to leave for the catch up.

*

The MOC meeting lasted an hour. Back at her desk,

Yiyun emailed its members a timetable of the Yellow Files Project.

'Anyone want anything?' Geoffrey said. 'I'm going downstairs.'

'No,' Yiyun said sharply. Then, remembering herself, she said, 'No, thank you.'

'Okay doke,' said Geoffrey and went on his way.

Yiyun inserted her blue memory stick and finally downloaded the files. One down. It took four minutes.

Geoffrey returned and started telling her about his younger brother, who he was disgusted with because he had cheated on his girlfriend.

At 10.30 the IT technician arrived to fix Betsy's computer. When she was through, she wanted to know what Yiyun had done to access Betsy's profile, because back on Betsy's home computer there was some snag.

Not long after that Tasha called to see what time Yiyun was going to lunch. Yiyun said she was staying at her desk and having a short one.

A little later Orson came by, as loud and as funny as ever, and entertained the troops for a while before handing Geoffrey the stationery he'd ordered and going on his way.

And in between all of this, doggedly, determinedly, like the committed revolutionary she was, Yiyun downloaded data incriminating the President and exposing hypocrisy at the heart of government onto multi-coloured memory sticks and dropped them into her bag.

By lunchtime, against all the odds, she had done them all. As the office thinned out or people unloaded sandwiches onto their desks, Yiyun picked up her bag, took the stairs to the sixth floor and walked to a thin door with a broken handle that couldn't lock. On the other side of the door was the stationery cupboard, a narrow galley that could just about comfortably fit three people. She closed the door behind her and pushed a box of printing paper against it to hold it shut. She reached up and claimed a stack of small jiffy bags from the top shelf. Then she set about the steady task of placing a memory stick in each bag, sealing it and shoving the jiffy straight into her rucksack. She was almost finished when she heard the hiss of the box of paper being pushed across the floor as someone opened the cupboard. When whoever it was felt resistance, they hesitated.

'Hello?' a voice said.

'Hello,' Yiyun said in a friendly way.

The door opened. Bhaskar, a quiet, middle-aged researcher from the Policy Unit blinked at the box on the floor.

Yiyun didn't know anything about Bhaskar other than his name.

'The door was swinging open and getting in the way,' she told him.

Bhaskar entered the cupboard and closed the door experimentally behind him. It clicked into place.

Yiyun had three jiffy bags left to do.

'Seems alright now,' Bhaskar said.

Yiyun shrugged.

'I wish they'd fix that handle,' Bhaskar added.

He looked over Yiyun's shoulder to the back wall.

'I need a couple of binders,' he said.

Yiyun turned to look.

'What colour?'

'What colours are there?'

'Red, blue, green and black.'

'Oh, black,' Bhaskar said. 'Better look professional, it's for Oxley.'

Yiyun handed him two black binders. Then she looked thoughtfully upwards as though considering the range of envelopes available to her.

'Thank you, um…' Bhaskar said.

'Yiyun,' she told him.

'Thank you, Yiyun,' the researcher said and left her to it.

For a second Yiyun pictured Bhaskar giving evidence at her prosecution. *Days before the media received the leaked material, I saw her loitering in the stationery cupboard on the sixth floor of the Department of Social Welfare. She was holding a jiffy bag identical to Exhibit A.*

She filled her final three jiffy bags in peace. Then she sat on a footstool in the corner and pulled a sheet of labels from her bag. Methodically, she applied a label to each jiffy. She found herself enjoying it – it reminded her of her first job when she was eighteen, for Room, the payer housing charity that was banned two months ago. When she was finished, she slipped her rucksack onto her shoulder and left the cupboard, returning to the stairs and walking all the way to the ground floor and out of the building.

*

Outside, the sun was shining. She had thought her drone might be wrongfooted by her appearance (she rarely left the building during the day), but it clocked her immediately.

She walked briskly but (she hoped) normally. The Post Office was only five minutes away, but she stopped at a café for a wrap and then lingered in a Busters and bought two birthday cards. At the Post Office, her drone waited outside alone – not many government employees or other suspects using the mail today. The franking machines were away from the window, hidden from the drone's view, but the Post Office cameras were on her the whole time. As Yiyun stamped and posted twenty little jiffy bags containing data that could scoop out the heart of the government, the government watched her do it.

She dropped the jiffys through the slot one at a time. Then she dropped the two birthday cards in after them, sealed and paid for – a small gesture towards throwing the cameras off the scent a little. The Policy hadn't asked her to do that, it was a touch of her own.

Yiyun shuffled her bag back onto her shoulder and walked outside. She didn't need to tell anyone what she had done: the Policy would see the results. She suddenly felt very free. She didn't want to go back to work, so she called Tasha, who answered from her desk with a mouthful of falafel.

'Hey,' Yiyun said. 'I changed my mind. Fancy going for a walk? It's a lovely day.'

12. OTTOLINE

One week after Yiyun's visit to the Post Office, Ottoline Middlebrook called in at Rawlins Books. Her friends were waiting for her. Glynis had arrived first thing to help open up, but neither she nor Ottoline had a shift that day; Krystan and Sanford had come in with her and had just hung around. The shop was empty, but in the café a little crowd of a dozen or so had gathered around a little black and white TV that Mr. Rawlins had set up on a table. Mr. Rawlins himself was amongst them, standing slightly apart, very quietly and with an unreadable expression.

The crowd stood around the TV in a rough kind of semi-circle and Glynis and the others were at the near end as Ottoline approached. They were watching the news. Ottoline tugged on Glynis's shoulder and her friend turned and smiled, then hugged her. 'Oh, hey,' she said. Krystan and Sanford turned briefly to offer quick smiles before their eyes went back to the TV.

It was a warm May day, but Ottoline persisted as always with her motorbike jacket. Here in the store, however, she finally relented and hung it over a chair before joining the others in gluing her eyes to the screen.

A voice was talking over footage of a large crowd in Parliament Square – yesterday's crowd. Then it switched to show an even larger crowd in the square this morning, circled by neat rows of police androids and clouded over by an even spread of drones. The picture switched again to the presenter – Ottoline didn't recognise her, she didn't normally watch this channel – repeating updates about a lack of government statements and the total mystery surrounding the President's whereabouts and what she might do. A murmur of cynicism and anger purred through the café's little audience, even though none of this was news to anybody.

Today was day three. On day one, as the leak was first revealed, small groups had spontaneously appeared on Whitehall and outside Parliament and steadily grown, menacingly watched by drones, red drones and armed androids. On day two Justice and others got involved: what had begun as a burst of natural anger began to be organised. By the evening Parliament Square was full and the androids were issuing orders to disperse and firing warning shots into the air. But the drones did not attack as they had last year. People dispersed, peacefully enough – but this morning they were back in even greater numbers.

The leak erupted from multiple sources on the same day: Four, then EBC, then NationWatch had spilled breaking news that three months earlier President Houghton had been designated to pay the Price – and that the government

181

had responded by reversing the designation and covering it up. An anonymous whistleblower had posted irrefutable evidence (CDC records, government records, data direct from the EOC 2) to multiple news outlets. Later that day, Justice revealed that they, too, had been sent this evidence. The data was tested and verified and by the following day it was everywhere – even the most pro-PON papers were talking about it, because this wasn't about the Price itself: it was about hypocrisy.

Over the course of two days, as a kind of mania of chatter and anger exploded across every TV in England, the PON and its apologists began to crank out their response. At first the government dismissed the leaked data as false, but that didn't last long. Then they claimed that the designation had been made, but the President never informed – that didn't last long either, because of the record of the android witness. These responses were issued as written statements; nobody in government had confidence enough in them to go to a TV studio and push them out of their mouths. Then the government put it about that the designation had been the result of sabotage. Which only raised the question: what other designations had been the result of sabotage? How easy was it to compromise the EOC 2? Was the system *broken*?

The government quickly retracted that claim and sent Leandro Farringdon, Head of the Ministry of Citizenship, before the cameras to tell the country (and the world) that the government did not know how the President had come to pay the Price or how (or why) it had been reversed, but that they were investigating. He asked people to be patient while the government tried to get to the bottom of it.

From the moment the leak broke, Ottoline bought newspapers she'd given up on long ago, to see with her own eyes what angle they took, what excuses they made. She had a stash of papers in her room that she felt she would keep forever, however things turned out. The arguments put out by the PON's defenders amazed her. Their main line was to focus (in spite of the government's formal retraction) on the claim of sabotage, and to fill pages and pages with scarifying stories about Justice, the Dream League, the Werkers, and a semi-mythical group of subversives at the heart of government itself, the Policy of Truth. The nation was threatened, they warned, not by the reversal and cover-up of the President's payment but by the shadowy, dangerous forces of disorder within the government and across the country – the pockets of revolution and chaos that thrived unchecked. In reality the worst thing the government had done, they argued, was allow these groups to grow for so long. The real problem was that for the past decade or so the PON had been too soft.

But by day two many of these papers' readers were already out on the streets, so they tried other angles. The President should never have been made to pay the Price in the first place: it was disorderly to have the country's leader in such a vulnerable position. The government had done the right thing, for the good of the nation, in correcting this weakness – this whole episode exposed an oversight in the Price's implementation. Other commentators, in the same pages, had a softer take: yes, this was bad, but it was understandable given the President's position and responsibilities – she should apologise, and that should be the end of the matter. A review should be conducted to establish how potential future designations of senior ministers should be dealt with; we may not want to go so far as to alter the EOC 2's programming, but perhaps certain senior figures should be granted immunity from payment, for the sake of national stability? This led to a whole debate about where the line should be drawn: if senior ministers were given immunity, why not senior civil servants? Farringdon was asked on live TV whether he felt he should have it – he demurred. And if ministers and civil servants, why not senior business leaders? Generals? Landowners? Who, exactly, should be shielded from the Price? (Everyone! Ottoline said to herself). It undermined the principle of arbitrariness; it undermined the whole policy. Ottoline loved it, how they tangled themselves in knots trying to protect themselves from the system they were defending. Meanwhile, many in the League claimed that the Price was already rigged – that was how the government knew it was sabotage.

There were a couple of hesitant voices suggesting that perhaps the President should resign, for the sake of national unity. But they did not suggest – no one suggested – that she should pay the Price.

Meanwhile the streets filled. Crowds gathered in town squares and high streets, outside council offices and police stations. It was as though something snapped: after decades of fear, decades of insecurity, decades of accepting the PON's order through fear of chaos, suddenly, hearing that the President herself had cheated the system, millions had had enough.

Flicking through her new collection of historical

editions of the papers, Ottoline discovered that some of the press had taken advantage of the confusion to print things they would never normally have bothered with, or dared to publish. Justice members and Liberals were given whole pages. Even the reaction of the Dream League got space, reported second hand and always with the prefix 'revolutionary group' or 'anti-Price faction' – but their words were there. What everyone said was entirely predictable. Justice called for reform of the Price, for a universal economics based on deserving; the Liberals merely called for greater transparency in how the Price operated. Both wanted Houghton to resign but, like the PON's defenders, neither thought she should be made to pay. The Dream League didn't care whether she resigned or not. Who cares, an unnamed protestor was quoted as saying, the whole system is rotten, bring the whole thing crashing down. Abolish the Price. Make everyone a citizen. Who cares about Houghton?

That was how Ottoline felt. She hoped, she hoped so much, that this scandal was the crack in the wall that would bring the PON down. It was time. This was their chance.

Today, day three, the streets were filling even more than before. She had been at Parliament Square yesterday, and she was going again today.

'We should get a move on,' Glynis said, turning from the TV, which was showing screenshots of the leaked data for the millionth time.

'Yes,' said Ottoline, picking up her jacket and folding it over her arm.

Krystan and Sanford, both of whom seemed to have

fallen into trances, shook themselves and placed half-finished bottles of lemonade on the table.

'Alright,' said Sanford.

They nudged a couple of elbows to say goodbye to people they knew and left the shop. Mr. Rawlins nodded very slowly as they passed him by. 'See you later,' he said, in a way that left them uncertain whether he meant back in the shop or out on the streets.

In the fresh air Ottoline scrambled back inside her motorbike jacket. With the bookstore behind them they turned right and walked the twenty minutes to Turpin Station. These days Ottoline, Glynis and Krystan had five drones each and Sanford had eight, crowded above them like a bad mood. When it rained they actually functioned quite well as umbrellas. They walked in silence, as they always did now when outdoors, with the drones watching them so closely. Sanford had a rucksack hitched to his back, but the others carried only tote bags loaded with flasks of water and snacks. At the station they walked through the gates and down the stairs, leaving their drones behind.

On the platform they slipped into their health masks and were free to talk again in low voices. The platform was pretty busy and Krystan wondered if everyone was going where they were. There was a buzz in the air, an excitement, that the four of them felt as the electricity of a government about to fall.

A tube arrived and they stepped on board, shuffling as part of the crowd and finding standing room only. They held onto straps in the central aisle and swayed as the train moved. After a minute Sanford said:

'Where do you think Houghton is now?'

They thought it over. It was an intriguing question that everyone was asking; they had discussed it themselves a lot, but Sanford never grew tired of talking about it. Those closest to them in the packed aisle listened curiously.

'Holding up in Downing Street freaking out,' said Krystan.

'She could have left the country,' Glynis offered.

'Hiding in Chequers,' Ottoline suggested.

These were all good and plausible speculations. Sanford didn't have anything better. The President hadn't been seen or heard from since the leak.

'It's so strange,' Sanford said.

'It's the Policy of Truth,' Ottoline said. 'It's messed them up.'

'She doesn't know what else they've got,' said Glynis.

Krystan nodded.

'I'm still surprised,' Sanford said. 'I thought they'd be more aggressive.'

'They're on the backfoot,' his brother told him.

'Do you really think she's gone abroad?' Ottoline asked Glynis.

Her friend shrugged.

'I don't know. It would make sense to me... don't busted dictators usually flee the country?'

Ottoline laughed.

'I suppose so.'

'She's definitely busted,' Sanford said. 'Whatever happens to the PON, she's done for.'

They fell quiet and the time came to change trains. The little gang disembarked, walked a short corridor to a train helpfully waiting, and stepped on board the Jubilee Line.

This train was even busier than the first – too busy to talk easily, so they didn't bother trying. A couple of stops along the way, Sanford wriggled his rucksack from his back and pulled out a clutch of pamphlets.

'The truth about the Price,' he said, raising his voice, and began handing them out to the people immediately around him.

'Sanford…' his brother said quietly, nervously.

But people were taking them, briefly smiling or nodding at Sanford or at one of the others. Some passed them along the carriage. Someone giggled.

'Plenty more where those came from!' Sanford said. He passed wads of his handiwork to Ottoline, Krystan and Glynis, who began to distribute them in human chains along the train. The carriage grew loud with murmurs and then open talk and laughter as passengers shared pamphlets and began discussing what was happening, between friends, between strangers.

'Down with the PON!' someone shouted.

'Down with the Price!' a young woman added.

The carriage cheered. The little gang exchanged glances with wide eyes.

The train lurched into Westminster Station and almost everyone heaved en masse towards the escalators. Without the anonymity of being packed together on the tube, and with the better reach of the station's cameras, people grew quiet and pamphlets were swiftly tucked into bags and jackets. But the energy was still there, the station was filled with it.

At the top of the escalator Ottoline and her friends moved through the gates and up a short, wide flight of steps into the sunshine. Their drones were waiting for them. The ancient Palace of Westminster loomed in front and Parliament Square lay to their right.

The place was already filled with people. Ottoline had never seen so many. The gang walked the short way from the station and crossed the road to approach the square. The road itself was packed, a sea of citizens and payers that filled Whitehall all the way up to Downing Street and beyond. Outside Downing Street there was shouting and chanting, separate from the chanting and shouting filling the air outside the Palace. The crowd in Parliament Square was so large and so packed that all they could do was go around it. Every face was turned towards Parliament but there was no stage, no focal point, no leaders or speeches. Just the crowd and the government. Around the edges, like a perimeter fence, stood a row of silent androids, conspicuously armed and circling everything.

Ottoline inspected them nervously. Then she turned away to search for faces she recognised. Above the crowd, blocking the sunlight, lay a thick swarm of drones, static, watching – more drones than Ottoline had ever seen in one place. She pulled Sanford's arm and pointed.

'Look at them all!' she said. The drones were so tightly packed they seemed to form a single entity that could descend at any moment and squash the gathering below.

Sanford watched, sharing her amazement.

'I'm surprised they can see anything,' Ottoline said. 'They're just getting in each other's way.'

Then she noticed, with a cold intake of breath, that some of the drones had markings. Sanford noticed them too. He nudged Krystan and Glynis.

'Red drones,' he told them.

Ottoline examined the mass of people around them. They couldn't have been the only ones to have noticed. No one seemed to care.

There were a few placards among the protestors but not many – a handful of damp-stained League ones (Owen must be here somewhere! she thought) and a smattering of homemade efforts, mostly simple slogans scrawled onto brown cardboard in black ink, a few that were more inventive. From up ahead, chants rippled back untidily – the most frequent a furious 'Pay the Price!' launched at the President herself, or at everyone in the PON people now believed had been cheating them. What *did* the people here believe? Ottoline wondered. What did they want, exactly? Did they even know?

But other chants were rising up as well, chants Ottoline was happier to hear: 'Abolish the Price!' and most of all 'The Price is a lie!' These chants were quieter, more stilted than the first, as though they felt strange in people's mouths, but they were there, and growing stronger. Were they spontaneous, or were there Leaguers in the crowd starting them up? Whatever their source, they were what Ottoline wanted, what everyone needed. As those chants reached where she and her friends stood, finding themselves after all this time at the back, latecomers, she joined in.

'The Price is a lie!'

They stood like this for a long time. Parliament stood in front of them, impassive. What were they thinking, the people inside? Were they watching? What would become of this crowd, this anger? What would it – what would people – do next? What paths would they take? Who would emerge to lead them, and where? What would the PON do – retaliate, concede, negotiate, collapse?

Ottoline wanted the PON to fall and the Price to fall. She wanted it to end – the haves and the have-nots, the suppression, the denial of living to so many. She wanted something better to replace it and she hoped that today, now, she was seeing the old injustice crumble. She hoped the River of Life and the Dream League rose high in what followed: people like Sanford, like Krystan, like Glynis.

They stood in the crowd for a long time and the crowd grew, and all the while Parliament was silent. Then Ottoline noticed a movement among the drones, as though they were shifting their position, changing their formation. She watched them warily. Others noticed it too. The drones were thinning out, separating and spreading apart. The chanting stopped, the anger quietened, and everyone waited.

The drones hung silently for a few moments longer: then, in a single, synchronised movement, they left – narrowing into a stream that trailed over the rooftops of Whitehall and out of sight. Quicky, urgently, Ottoline turned to the androids surrounding the uprising. They were walking away. Their arms were at their sides, their weapons powered down.

Ottoline turned to her friends. She had tears in her eyes. She laughed.

ACKNOWLEDGEMENTS

Thank you to my wife, Jatinder Padda, the love of my life, who is also my first reader and creative collaborator, and the editor of this novel. Thanks also to: Polly Hawkins, Nick Barrow, Felicity Hawkins, Michael, Cristian, Dominic, Jenny, Bex, Archie, Oscar, Amelia, Isobel, Gurmej Padda, Swaran Padda, Gurpreet, Jagwinder, Matt, Anne, Alvar, and Sachin. Thanks to those who have supported this book or my attempts to write over the years: Blaine Greteman, Mandi Bozarth, Shonagh Musgrave, Sue Dance, Lucy Whitehead, Rob Whitehead, Becky Shah, Anne Haddican, Mike Brooks, Bob Chiang, Heidi Chiang, Meera Selva, Jeevan Vasagar, Kate Nevens, Alan Trotter, and Tristan Gray.